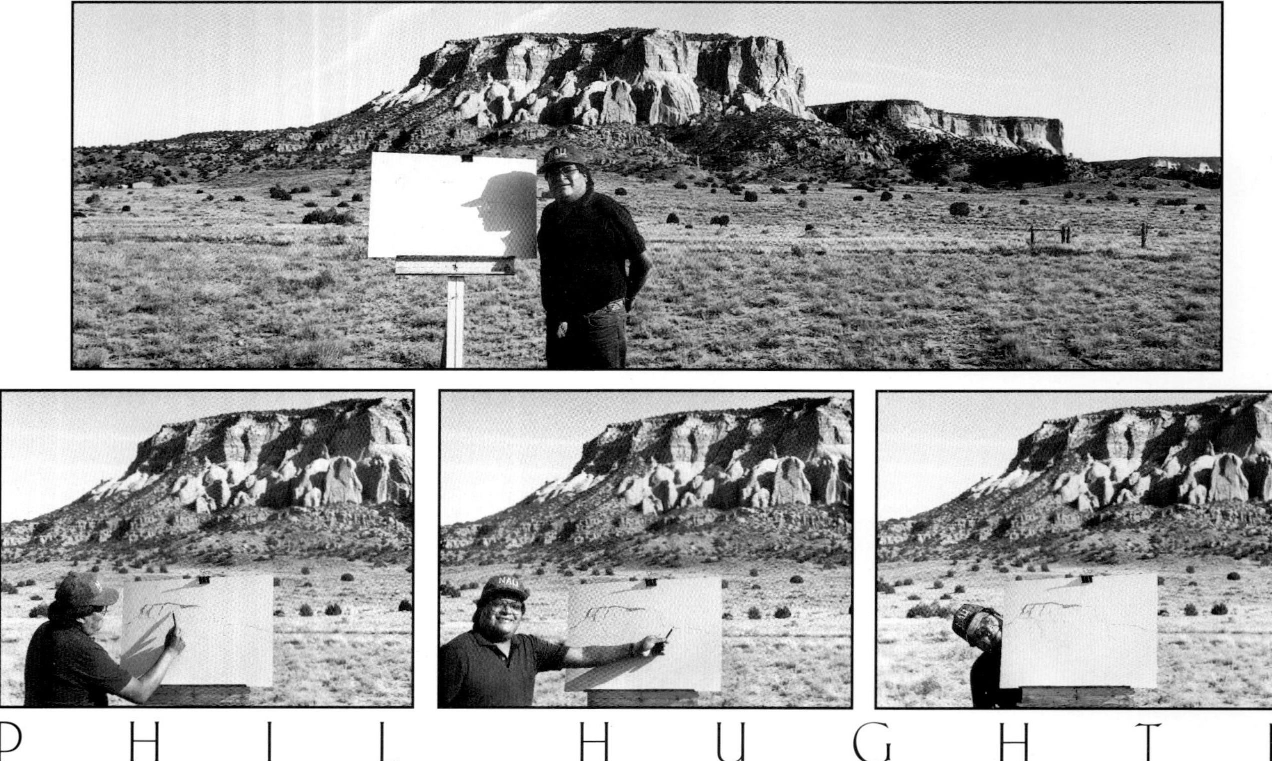


P H I L H U G H T E

# A Zuni Artist Looks At Frank Hamilton Cushing

CARTOONS BY PHIL HUGHTE

Publishers
Pueblo of Zuni Arts & Crafts
A:shiwi A:wan Museum and
Heritage Center

Designer / Typography
Anna María Chávez
Aztec Media Corp.

Printing
David Scates
Southwest Printing Inc.



Library of Congress Catalog Card
Number: 94-66486
**ISBN: 0-9641401-0-1**

Printed in the United States
of America on archival paper

---

Cover by Phil Hughte

# A Zuni Artist Looks At Frank Hamilton Cushing

## Cartoons by Phil Hughte

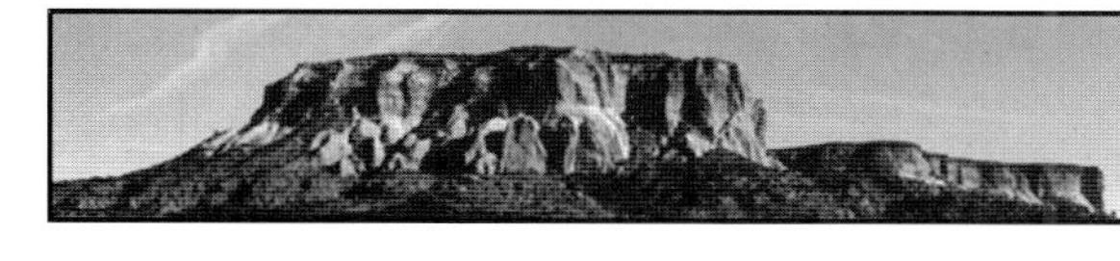

*Captions by Phil Hughte*

*Foreword by Triloki Nath Pandey*

*Discourse by Jim Ostler*

*Commentary by Krisztina Kosse*

Pueblo of Zuni Arts & Crafts ❂ Hwy. 53 ❂ Zuni, NM 87327
A:shiwi A:wan Museum and Heritage Center ❂ Hwy. 53 ❂ Zuni, NM 87327

# Contents

# Publisher's Note

Many projects begin with an idea about some issue to address or art to reveal. Then a grant is written, and a year and one half later (with some luck) the project kicks off. Notes are carefully made, photographs taken, interviews conducted, expenses itemized, time and budgets overrun, and an extension requested.

This book has a much simpler origin. It started with little effort: a quick conversation on Native American humor, and a request to Phil Hughte for some cartoons. Forty-three cartoons later, Phil felt he had covered the topic of Cushing.

The cartoons sat fallow for six months waiting for us to decide what to do with them. They were too good to sell, too good to break up. It was clearly a body of work that should stay together and be shared.

# Foreword

Phil Hughte began painting when he was seven years old in 1962. Two years later, when I met him in his grandmother's home, he impressed me as a sensitive and precocious boy. I noticed that he was very close to his grandfather, who was one of the important religious leaders of Zuni. I remember seeing Phil during the 1960s and '70s, whenever I visited with his grandfather. He never showed me any of his paintings or sketches, but his school teachers drew my attention to them. Along with some of his friends he often helped paint decorations for school events.

During the 1970s Zuni had a renaissance in jewelry making, pottery making and in artistic production in general, as one can see from *Zuni: the Art and the People* (volumes 1, 2 and 3 published between 1975 and 1977). Phil never took part in making jewelry since he found it "repetitive" and "restricting." He chose to use ballpoint pens and acrylic paints in drawing and painting "everyday life of his people," as he told me last summer. His school teachers and local traders encouraged his artistic endeavors.

While I was working on the Zuni land claim case during the early 1980s, I visited the pueblo quite often, but seldom saw Phil Hughte. I learned that he was away studying art at Northern Arizona University in Flagstaff. I continued to look for his paintings and occasionally saw a few with familiar themes such as women making bread at the outside ovens, snow falling on the sacred mountain Dowa Yalanne, and masked dancers *(kokko)* coming to Zuni. One of the high school teachers had a very good collection of Phil's paintings. Local trading stores also began to acquire his paintings and sketches about 1980.

With a Bachelor of Fine Arts degree from Northern Arizona University, in 1984, Phil joined Twin Buttes High School in Zuni. His steady work as art teacher brought him in contact with very creative students and faculty. He began painting and drawing a diverse range of subjects in a variety of media. He also began to read accounts of Zuni culture and society written by anthropologists, administrators, and missionaries. It was about eight years ago that Phil became interested in reading about the legendary anthropologist, Frank Hamilton Cushing (1857–1900), whose name he had heard from his grandfather. But it was one of his fellow teachers, Richard Brough, who told him about Cushing's works on Zuni. Phil was hooked; he found Cushing and his works quite "entertaining." The more he read, the more he realized that in Cushing he had found a subject for his artistic imagination. Even though Phil has been drawing cartoons for 15 years, it was only in the 1990s that he began to make the cartoons of Cushing we see in this book.

I think Phil says with his cartoons what I have attempted to say about Cushing in my paper "Anthropologists in Zuni" (1972). In these cartoons, the anthropologist is seen by the artist both as a fellow human being and as a professional scholar. In construing Cushing as a man in Zuni, the artist has chosen to emphasize his dress, his eating habits, his taking a bath, and his interaction with fellow Zuni men and women in the secular as well as sacred realms of life in the pueblo. He also comments on Cushing's marriage, settling with his wife and cook in Zuni, facing harsh winters, getting sick, and finally his "last supper;" eating a fish he choked on a fish bone and died on April 10, 1900.

In Phil's vision of Cushing as a professional anthropologist, we see him sketching Mudhead Kachinas, talking with informants, collecting pots and scalps, visiting the Hopi and the Havasupai, and taking his Zuni hosts to the East Coast to visit his friends and family. In his role as a Bow Priest, we see Cushing making prayer sticks, taking part in scalping an enemy, participating in the Scalp Dance celebrations, and protecting the Zuni against neighboring Navajo and Apache intruders as well as from fellow whites—missionaries, administrators, and traders—some of whom were robbing Zuni blind. Phil is exposing their greed by making Cushing challenge the land-grabbing activities of Senator John Logan (1826–1886) of Illinois and his son-in-law, Major W. F. Tucker, Jr. (see my paper, "Anthropologists in Zuni" for details).

Phil is also making us aware that Cushing's very presence was a disrupting factor in Zuni. His rivalry with fellow anthropologists (particularly James and Matilda Stevenson), his making of a Mudhead mask, and his meddling in pueblo politics contributed to ambivalence towards him in certain circles in Zuni. This is also supported by recent scholarly works on Cushing (see Readings).

Phil is well aware, as I became during the course of my fieldwork, that Cushing has become part of Zuni history. As an art teacher, Phil Hughte sees this exhibition and book as an educational opportunity for his people to learn about an important time in their history. For others, Phil sees this as a chance not only to get a glimpse of Native American-Anglo relations in Zuni, but also to see a side of Zuni art they have probably never imagined.

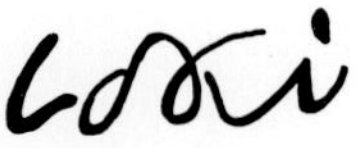

Triloki Nath Pandey
Professor of Anthropology
University of California, Santa Cruz

# The Cartoons

Phil Hughte's cartoons are organized chronologically. With few exceptions, the cartoons comment on real events. A handful are presumed by the artist to have taken place and, if they didn't, Phil believes that they should have.

The cartoons are accompanied by captions which were tape recorded by the artist and transcribed.

Sidebars adjacent to these captions compare the artist's interpretations with words written by Cushing or words written by others to or about Cushing. All quotes are taken from Green (1990) with the exception of those in the Filter Press edition of *My Adventures in Zuni* (1967).

# Young Cushing

*Cushing is doing his favorite hobby of making bows and arrows. His father is observing him and is so proud of young Cushing. Cushing got interested in Native American artifacts by finding an arrowhead in the back of his yard. And in this drawing there are so many artifacts that he had done. There is a picture of Andrew Johnson who was president when Cushing was ten years old.*

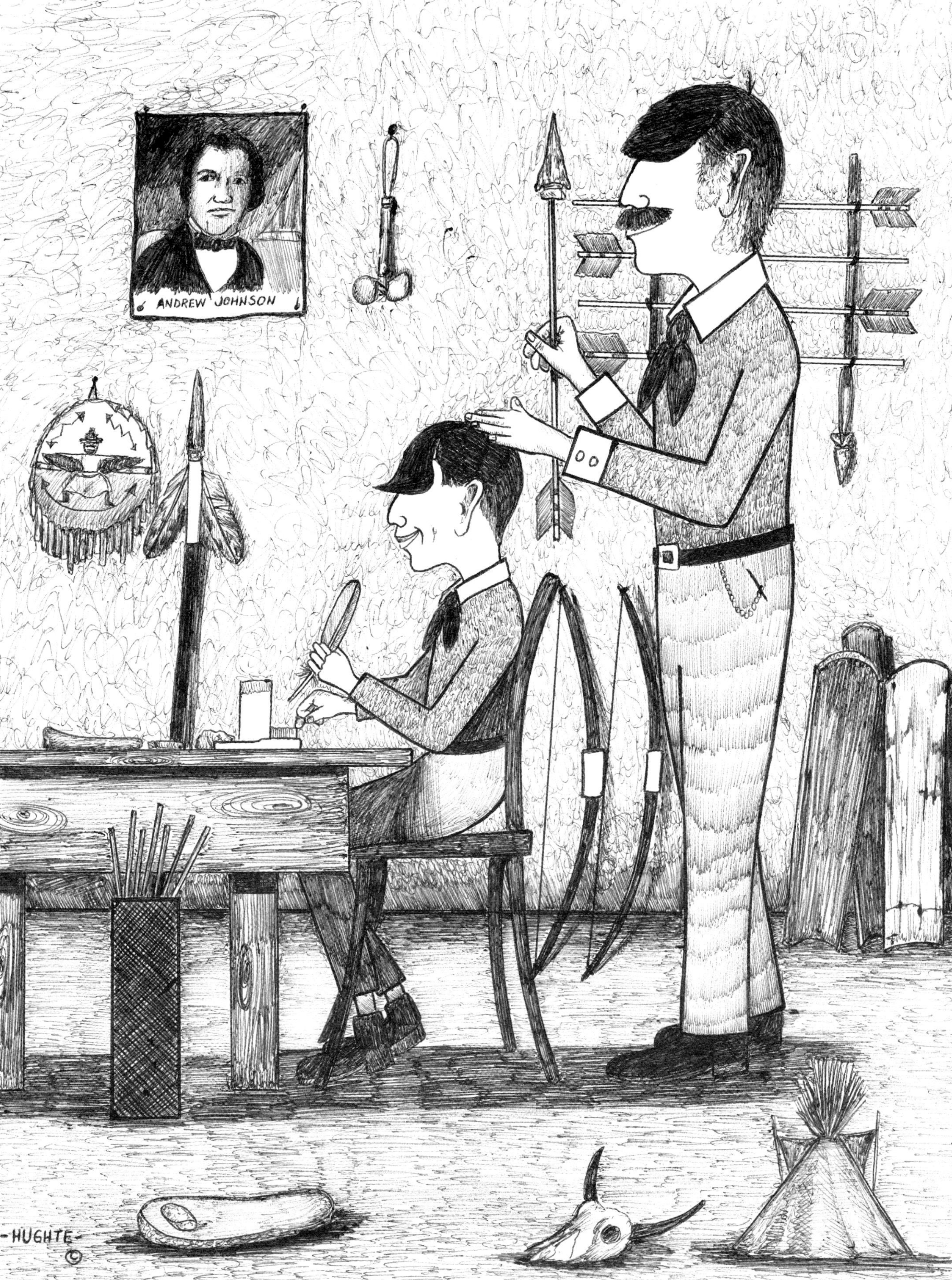
ANDREW JOHNSON
-HUGHTE-
©

Descending, I chanced to meet, over toward the river, an Indian. He was bare-headed, his hair banged even with his eyebrows in front, and done up in a neat knot behind, with long locks handing down either side . . .

I shook the proffered hand warmly, and said, "Zuni?"

—*My Adventures in Zuni*, p.2.

# Coming To Zuni—

*Cushing is coming to Zuni and the first person he meets is a sheep herder. According to his writings he describes the type of sheep and there was a dog and a Zuni just really looking at him.*

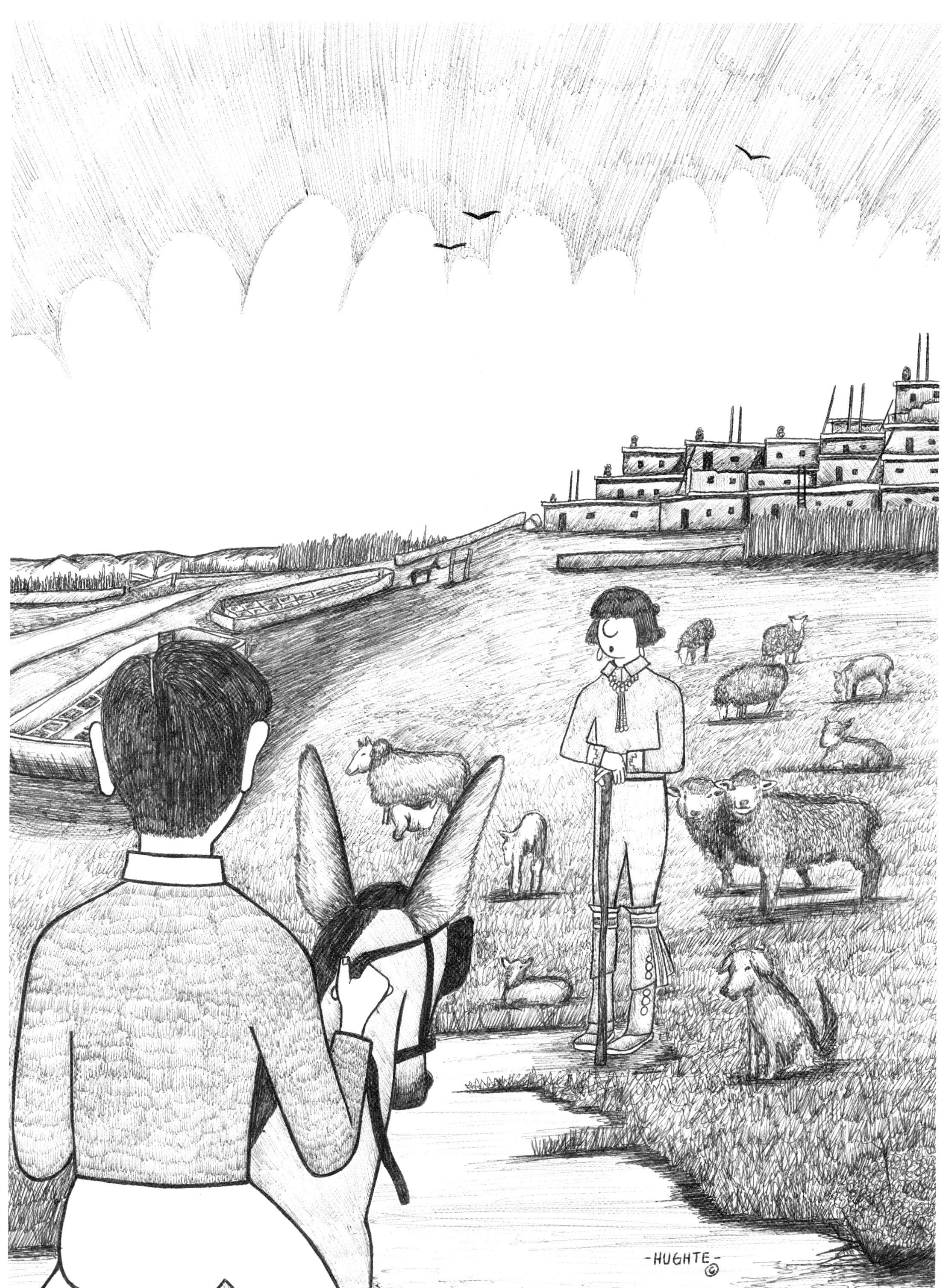
-HUGHTE-
©

# Eye To Eyes

*Cushing is coming to Zuni and everybody is looking at him. The first thing he sees is the Kachinas—the Mudheads. He describes in his writing the Kachinas with long beards and tongues sticking out, with young kids, all naked, chasing pigs. And that is what he sees when he comes to Zuni. A lot of Zunis started calling him "Washingdoon" which means that he was from Washington, D.C. and he was one of them politicians.*

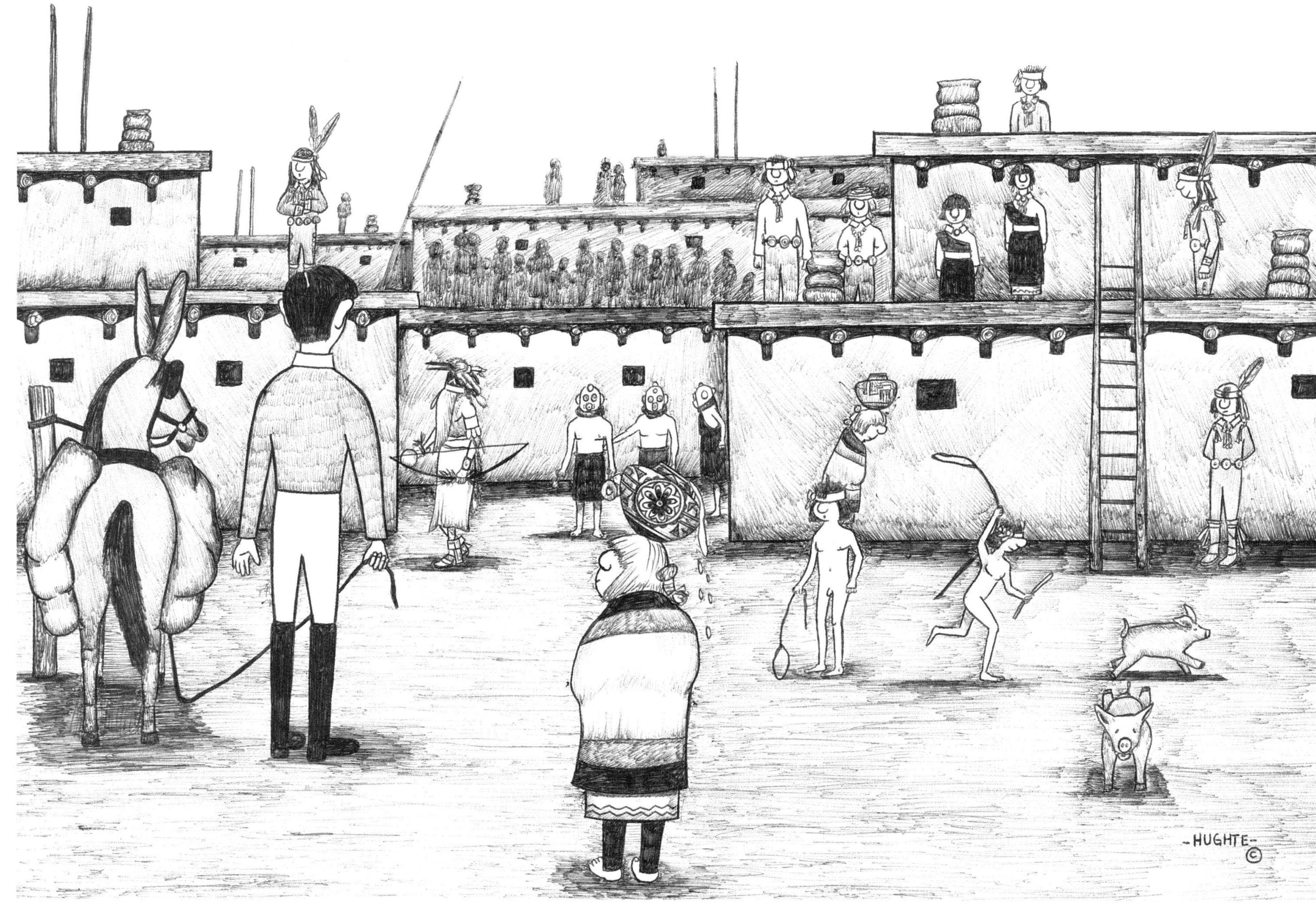
-HUGHTE-
©

The first time I appeared in the streets in full costume the Zunis were delighted. Little children gathered around me; old women patronizingly bestowed compliments on me as their "new son, the child of Wa-sin-to-na."

—*My Adventures in Zuni*, p.28.

## Becoming A Zuni —

*Zunis are making Cushing into one of their own people. They are taking the hammock away. And then the old lady brings his clothing and there is a young lady that is fixing him up with the traditional Zuni wear.*

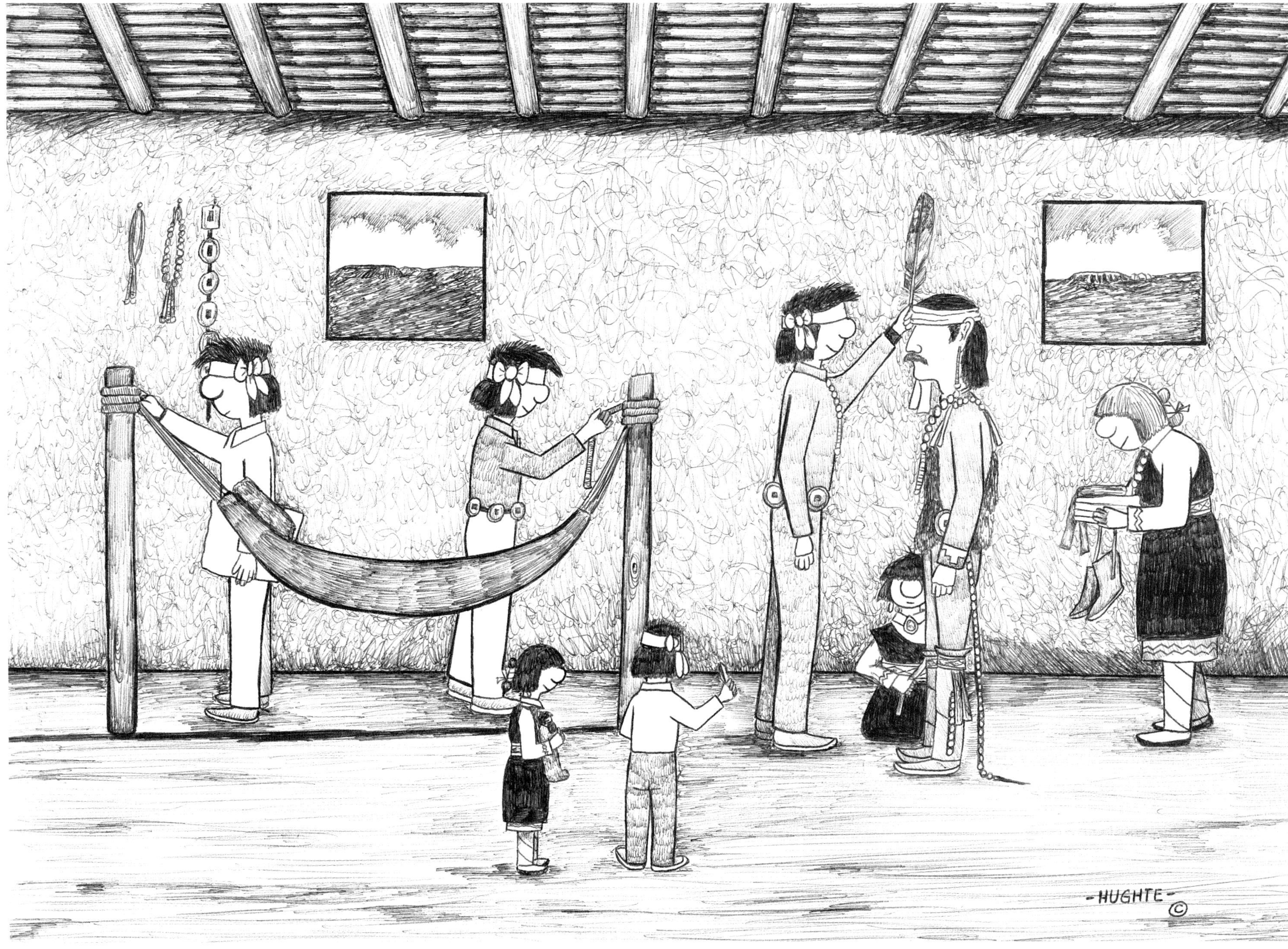
-HUGHTE-
©

# Small Leggings

*Cushing had such small legs where the traditional leggings wouldn't even go through the lady's fist. And kids are just making fun of him and the lady is at odds and wondering why so small.*

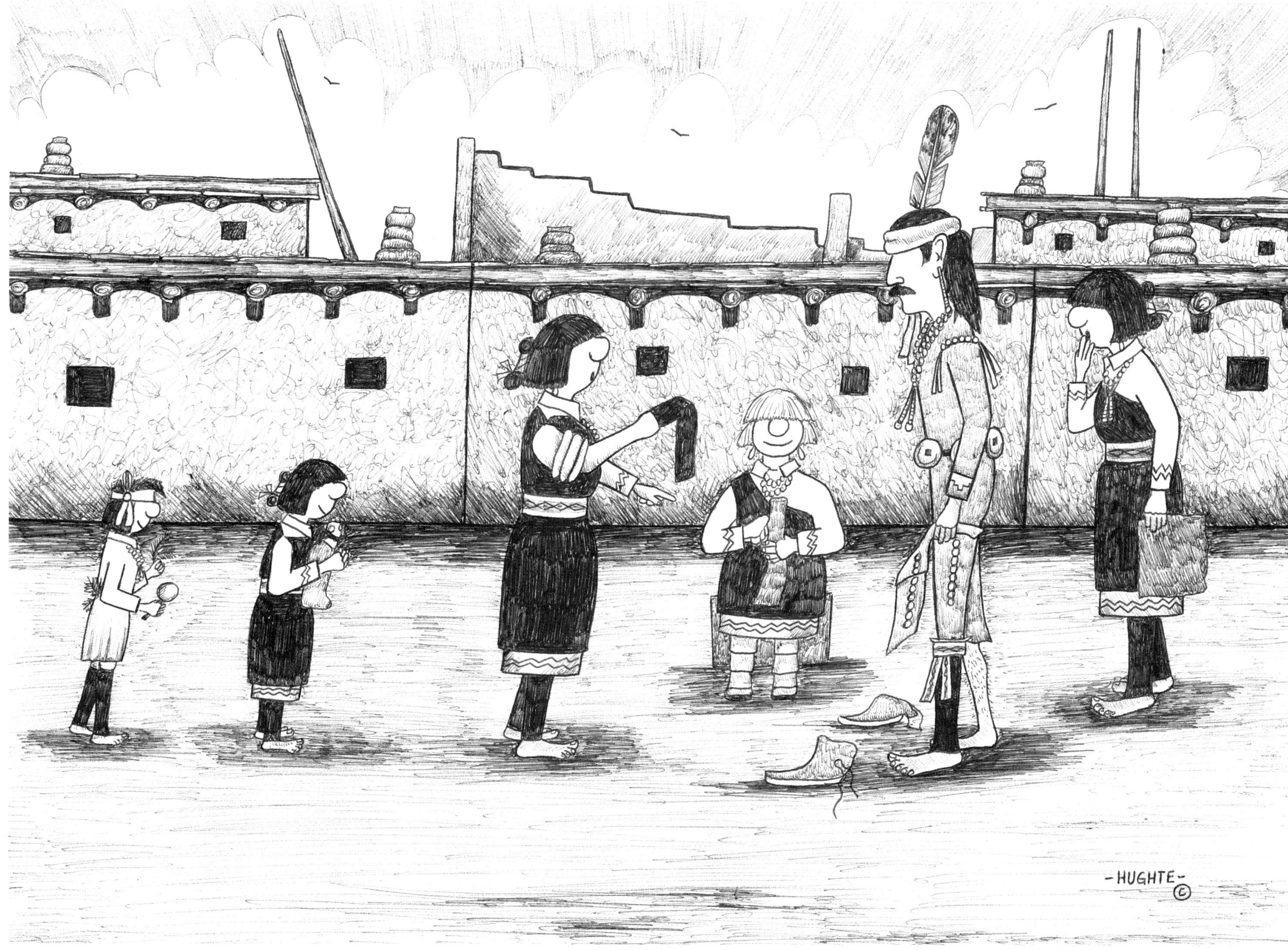
-HUGHTE-
©

Presently [Palowahtiwa] approached me, thrust two fingers under my chin, lifted up my face, and sawed across his stomach with the edge of his hand.

"Hungry?" said he.

"Yes."

"Very hungry?"

"Yes."

"Ha! Ha!"

Then he turned and caught sight of my bacon. He curled his lip contemptuously and pointed to it.

"Pig's grease?" said he.

"Yes."

"No good," he remarked in the first English I had ever heard him utter. . . .

—FHC lecture, December 10, 1890, Buffalo, New York.

# First Traditional Meal

*Cushing is ready to eat the Zuni traditional meal. He doesn't like the look of it and is thinking of his favorite meal—the fish.*

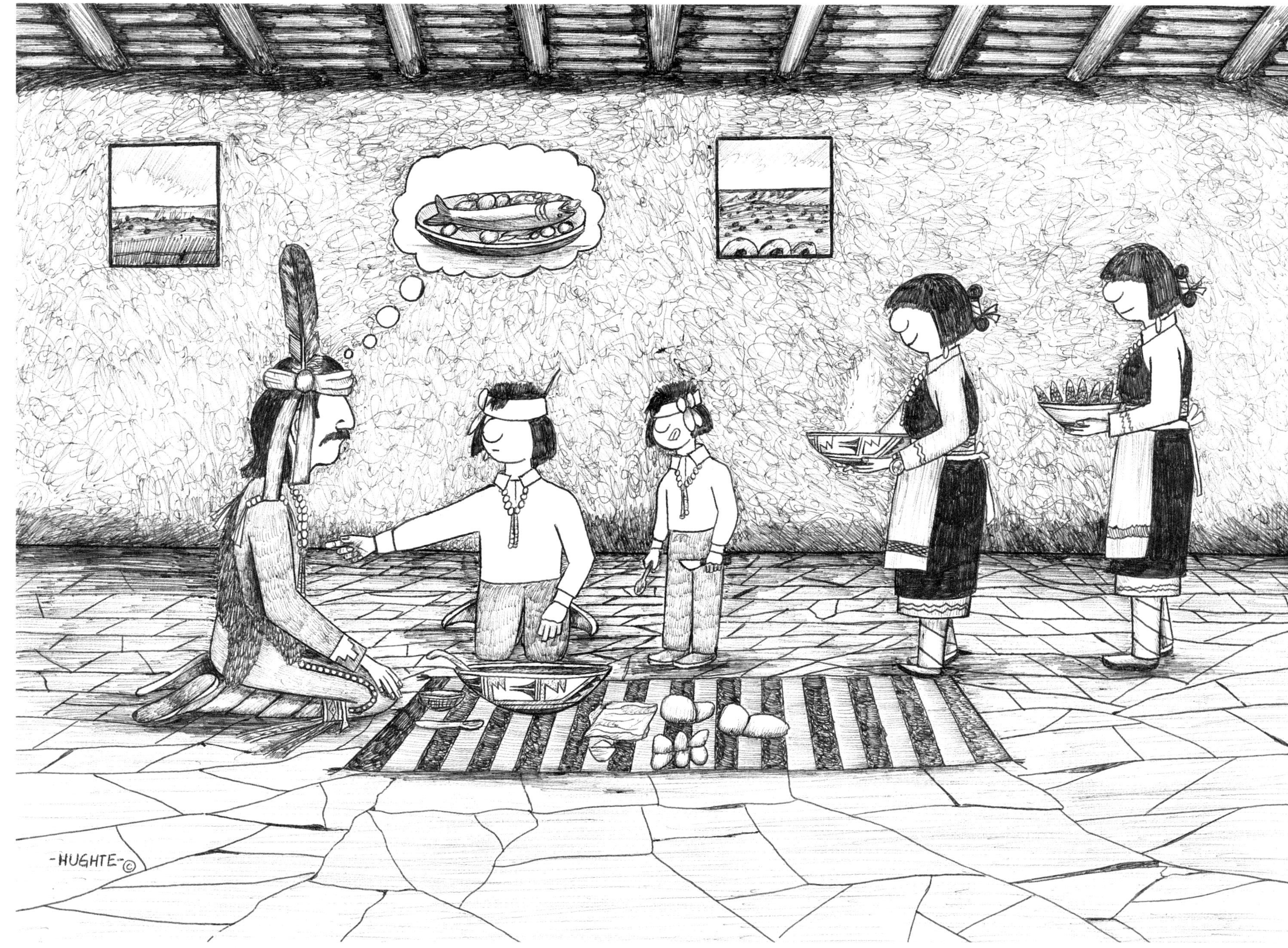
-HUGHTE-©

When I took my station on a house-top, sketch-books and colors in hand, I was surprised to see frowns and hear explosive, angry expostulations in every direction.

—*My Adventures in Zuni,* p.9.

# Please Don't Draw Us!

*Cushing went to watch the clowns perform and while he was observing he was drawing them. The Zunis saw what he was doing and they were hiding from him. They didn't want their faces to be drawn, and one clown is climbing up the ladder and is going after him.*

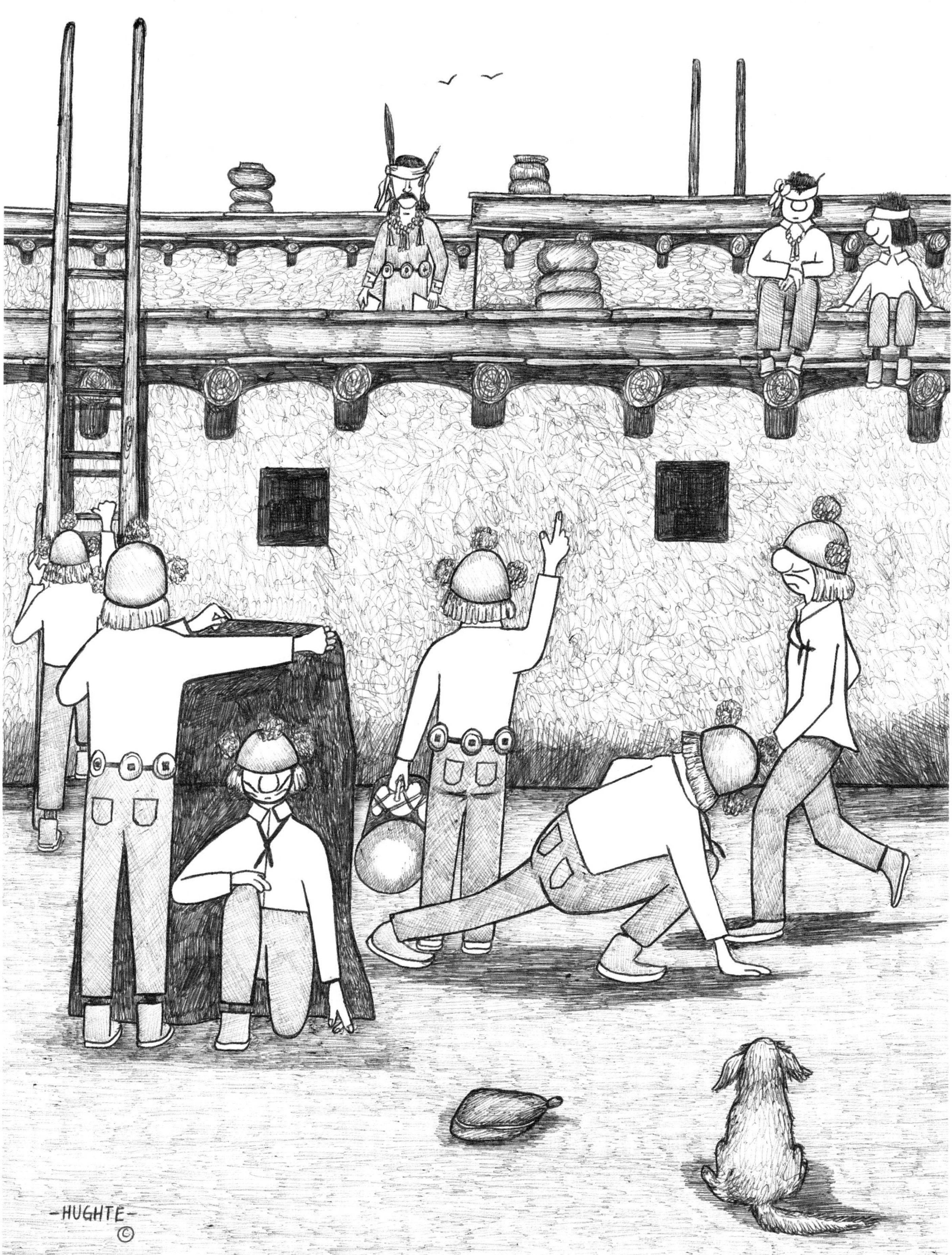
-HUGHTE-
©

## Judgment Day

*Here Cushing gets in trouble. He started drawing some religious artifacts and some of the religious leaders are after him. One wants to hang him, another wants to butcher him, while two bachelors want him to do nudes. And there is a young lady with her grandmother's painted pottery, and then on the right there is a Zuni who was caught for witchcraft and is being hanged.*

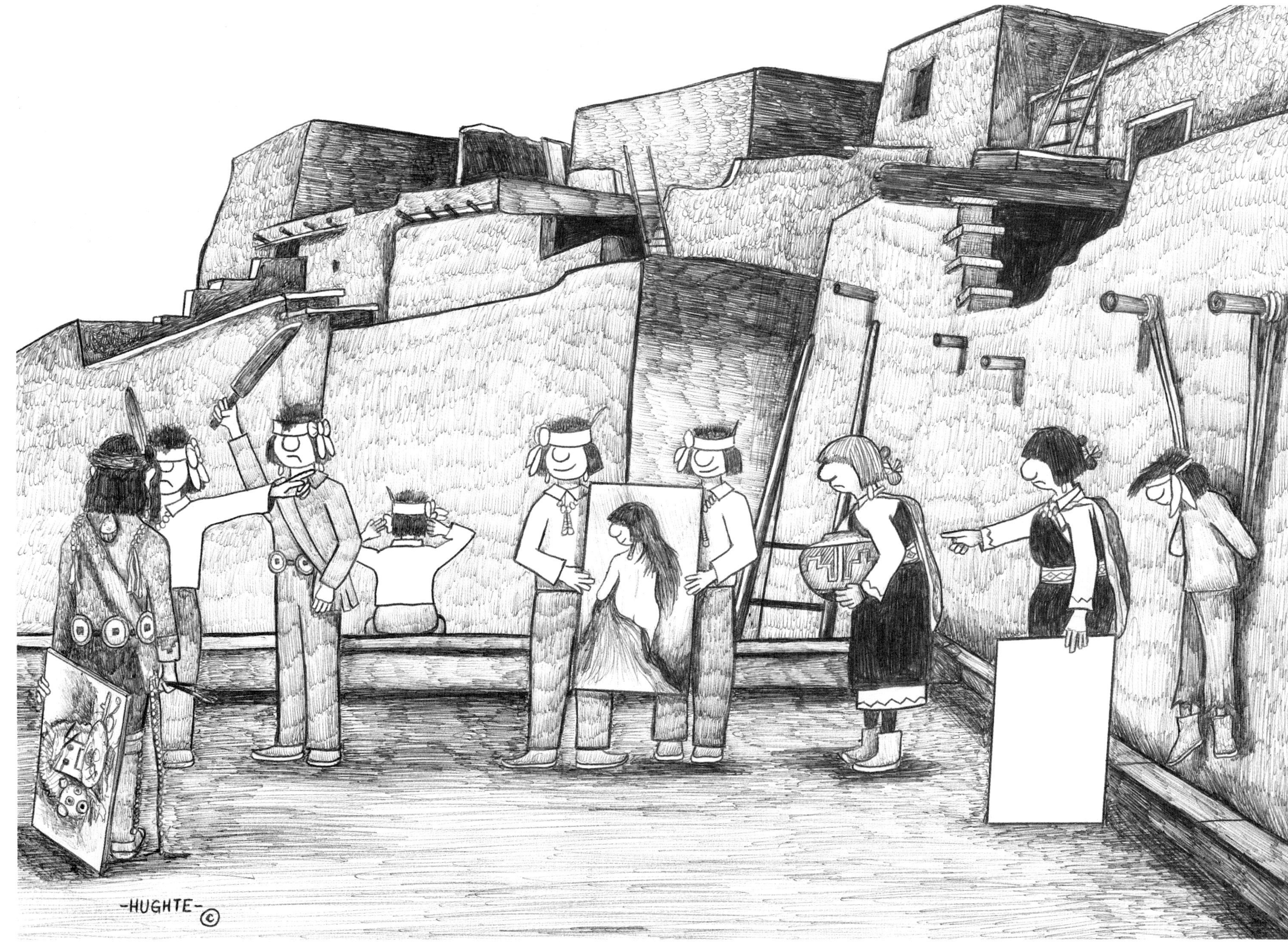
-HUGHTE- ©

# Here Cushing Meets We'wha

*Notice that she is very big. Cushing was pretty tall but We'wha was a lot bigger and stronger. We'wha was an artist and a farmer. Notice the weaving equipment on the wall. We'wha loved children so in this drawing I put children surrounding her.*

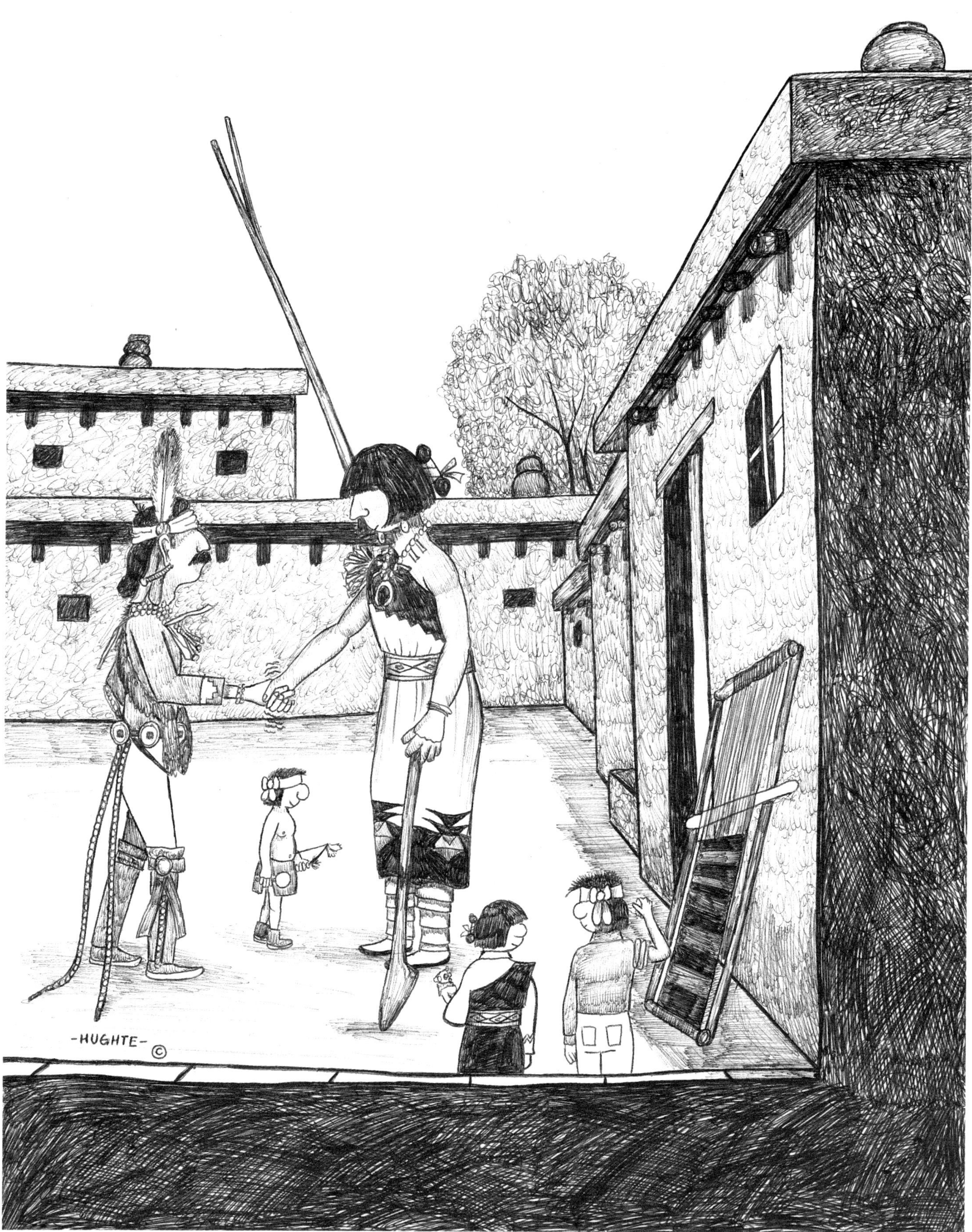
-HUGHTE- ©

May I, without offense, ask you once more to have shell matter and green stones sent? Especially imitation turquoise (which are very cheap at manufacturing jewelers). The request was well considered. It mean[s] almost *everything* regarding collecting among these Indians, and also much regarding my favor with them.

—FHC letter to Spencer Baird,
February 23, 1880.

## Have A Drink

*The clowns are playing tricks with* Cushing. *And here they are trying to have him drink urine. And the* Zunis *are just laughing and there is one young clown who is about to take the coins off his belt.*

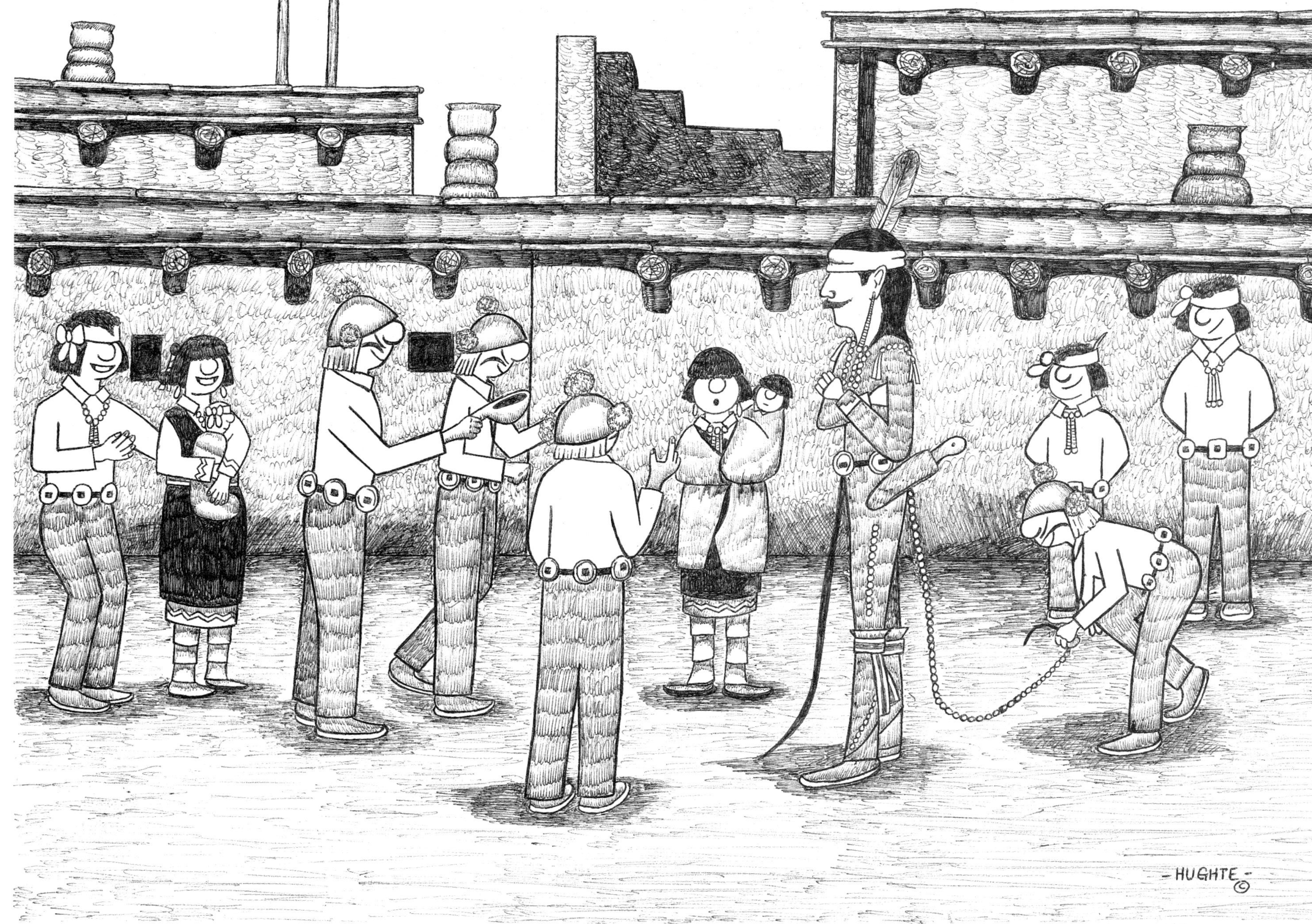
-HUGHTE-
©

# Picking The Lice—

*Cushing is getting his lice picked. A lot of Zunis used to do that before modern medicine and the ladies loved to do that. My grandmother used to love to do that to me when I was young. I just thought of this idea and I am sure that Cushing had lice when he was here.*

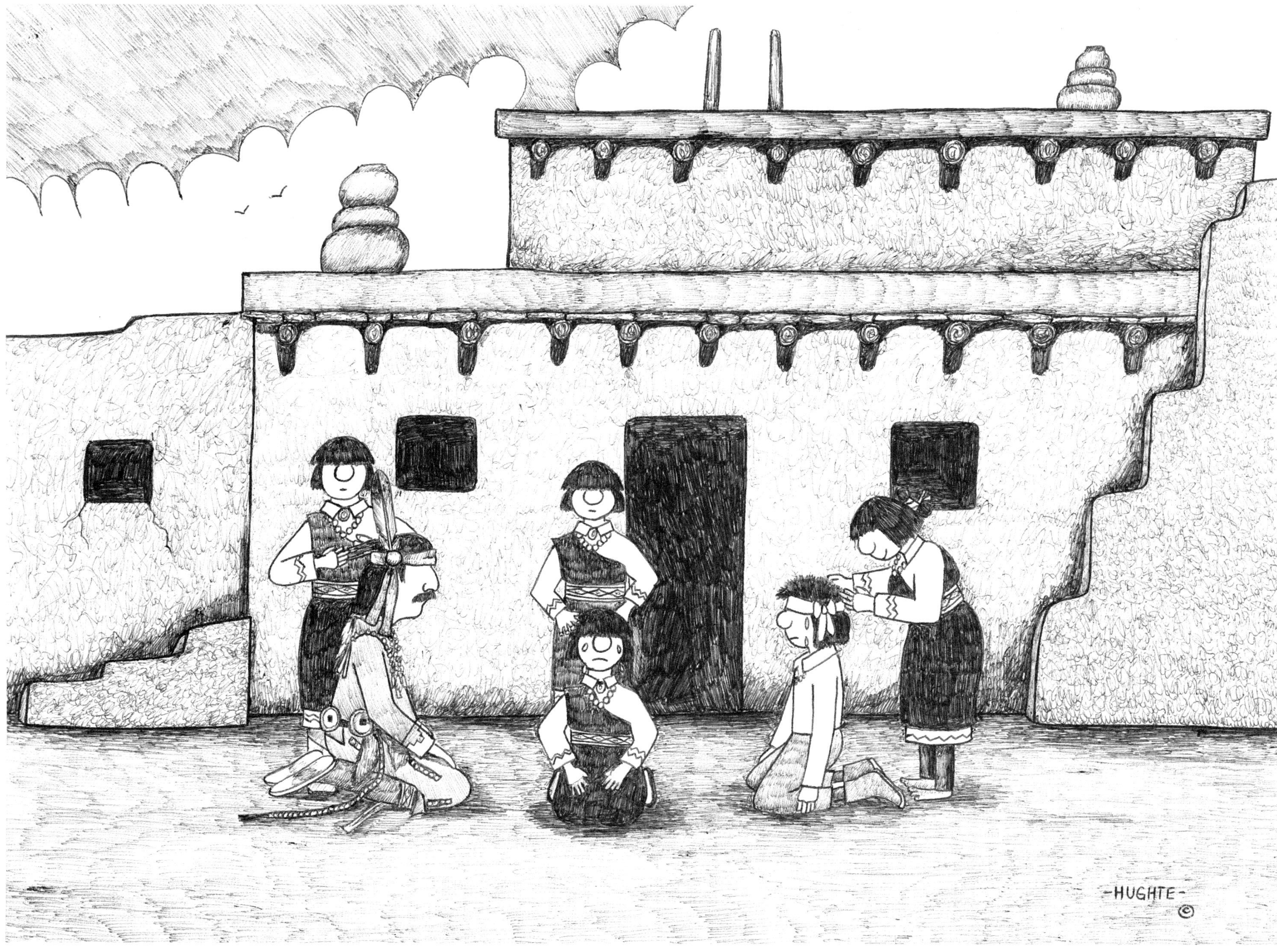
-HUGHTE-
©

# The Loud Musician

*Cushing was into everything and I am sure he played some type of Zuni instrument. Here he is blowing the flute and disrupting everybody. Matilda Coxe Stevenson is having a photograph taken of him and you notice that the dogs are all howling and the kids' ears are hurting and everybody's ears are hurting.*

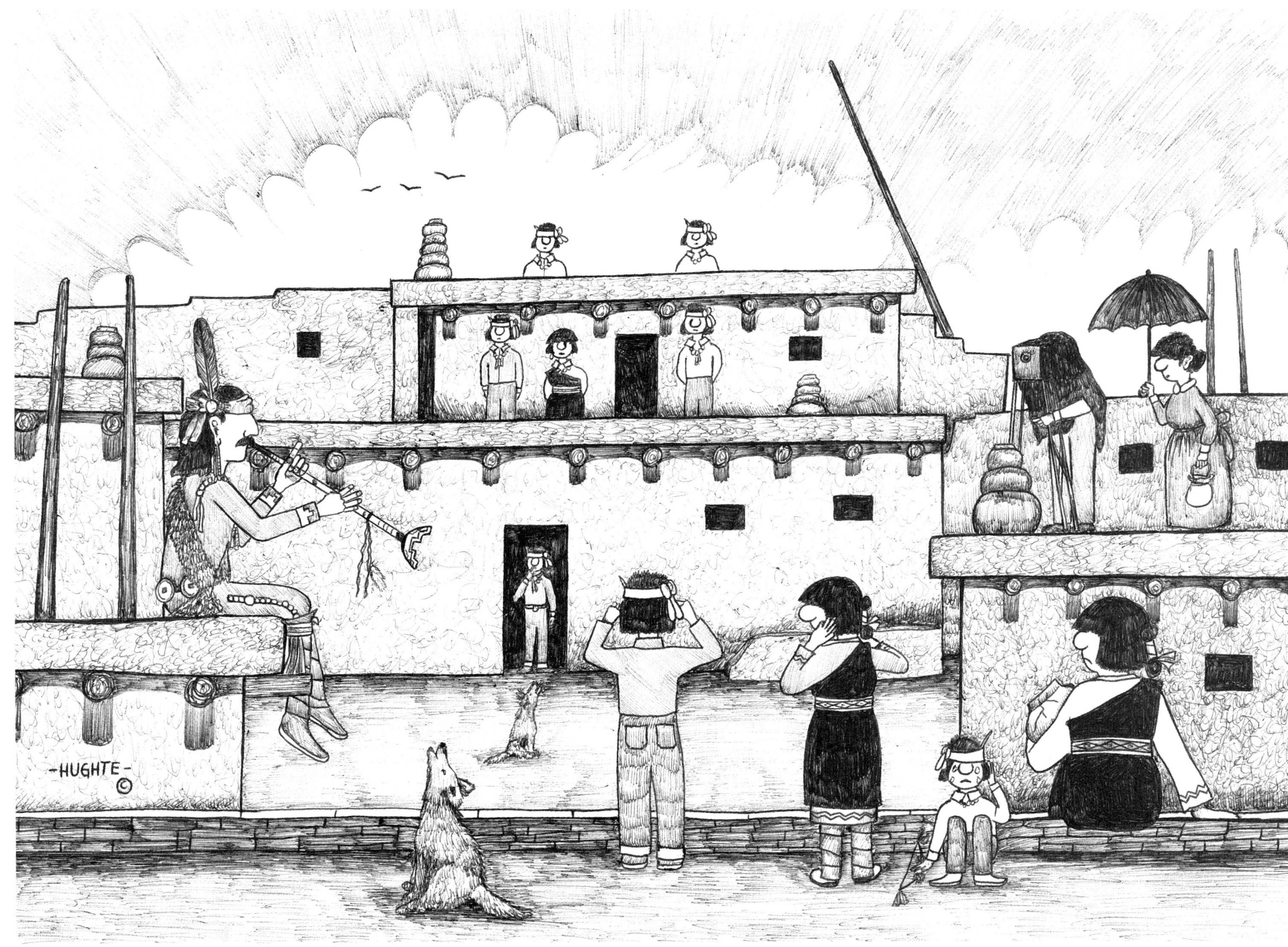
-HUGHTE-
©

But there was the wonderful addition [to Cushing's room in the governor's house] of a telephone which Mr. Cushing and his brother, who was visiting him, constructed out of a couple of old tin cans and several hundred yards of twine, to prove to the Zunis the truth of what he had told them about the triumphs of American invention.

—Sylvester Baxter in "The Father of the Pueblos," *Harpers New Monthly Magazine* 1882.

# Wrong Day To Bathe

*Cushing is taking his bath but there are three gossipers who are just gossiping away and Cushing is naked as a jaybird. On the right side there is a bull who is about to go after Cushing. Notice the soap and the traditional pit where they would take baths and on the other side, the left side, is the drinking area.*

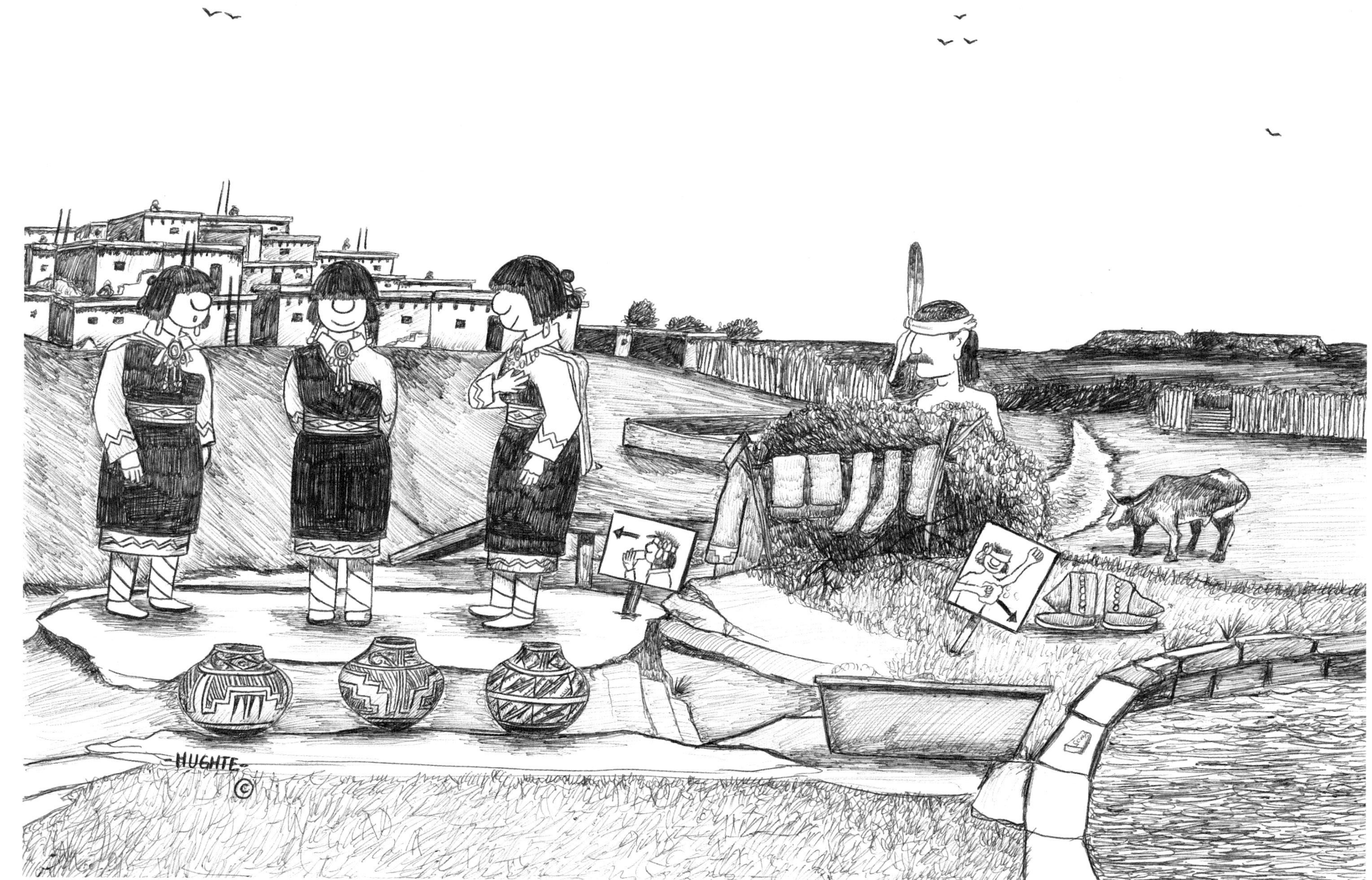
HUGHTE ©

# The Graffiti Clan—

*Cushing is writing his Zuni name and it has 1881 because that is when he became a Bow Priest. And what he did is that he gave some of the charcoal to the Zuni kids. All of a sudden they went bad and started putting graffiti everywhere and the boogeyman is coming after them.*

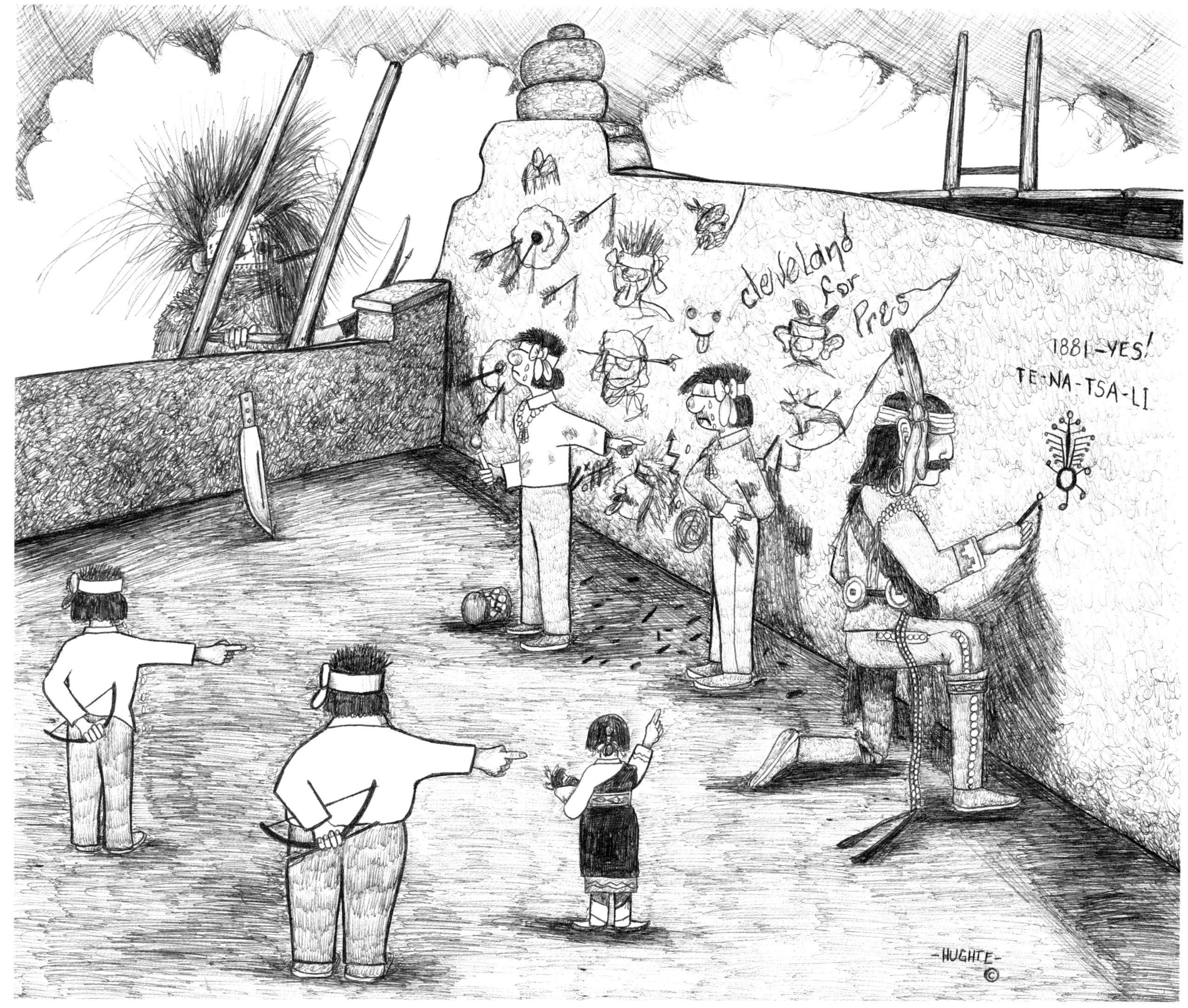
cleveland for Pres
1881—YES!
TE-NA-TSA-LI
-HUGHTE-
©

Dear Mr. Rhees:
I enclose herewith the vouchers [for payment of expenses] which you kindly sent. Do please be liberal with me. You do not know what I have suffered during this winter, nor how much that suffering would have been lessened by a more liberal allowance of means . . .

God bless you for your kindness to
Your humble friend.
F. H. Cushing

—FHC letter to William Rhees,
Chief Clerk of the Smithsonian.
February 23, 1880.

# Cold Winter

*Cushing couldn't take the winter months. So here Cushing is about ready to freeze and the rest of the Zunis are enjoying the subzero temperature. Kids are throwing snowballs at each other while a Zuni man is hauling wood and a lady is hauling water.*

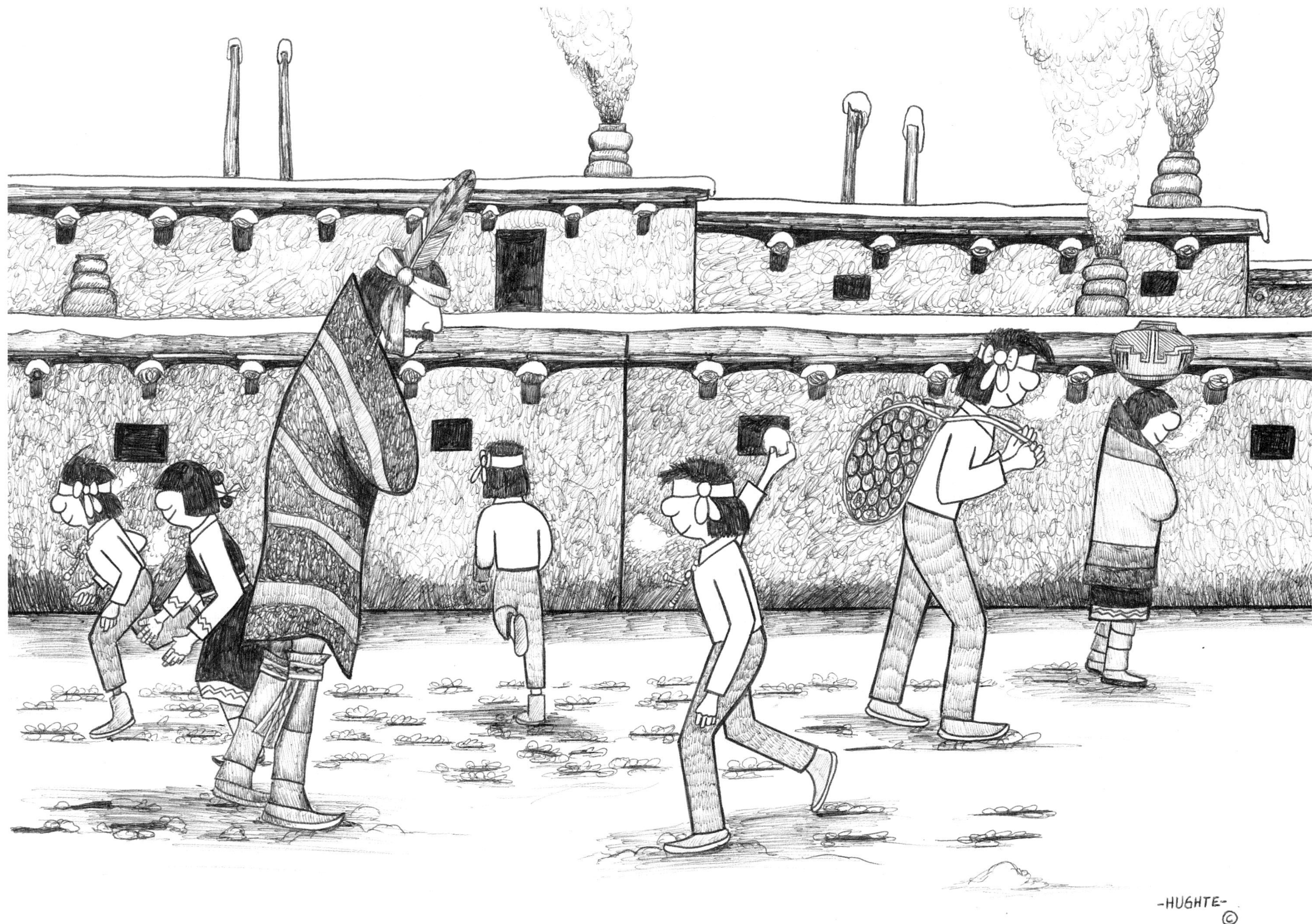
-HUGHTE-
©

# Sick Cushing

*Cushing has a hard time adjusting to Zuni life and used to get sick a lot. This is an illustration of Cushing getting sick. But he is not really sick, he just liked the idea of being pampered. Zunis are about ready to massage his stomach to comfort him, and two Zuni ladies are clipping his toe nails. And the other two ladies are bringing him food, and the Zuni man is going to put a new eagle feather on him because the old one is broken. Cushing is looking at two Zuni kids knowing that he is all right and he has his thumbs up.*

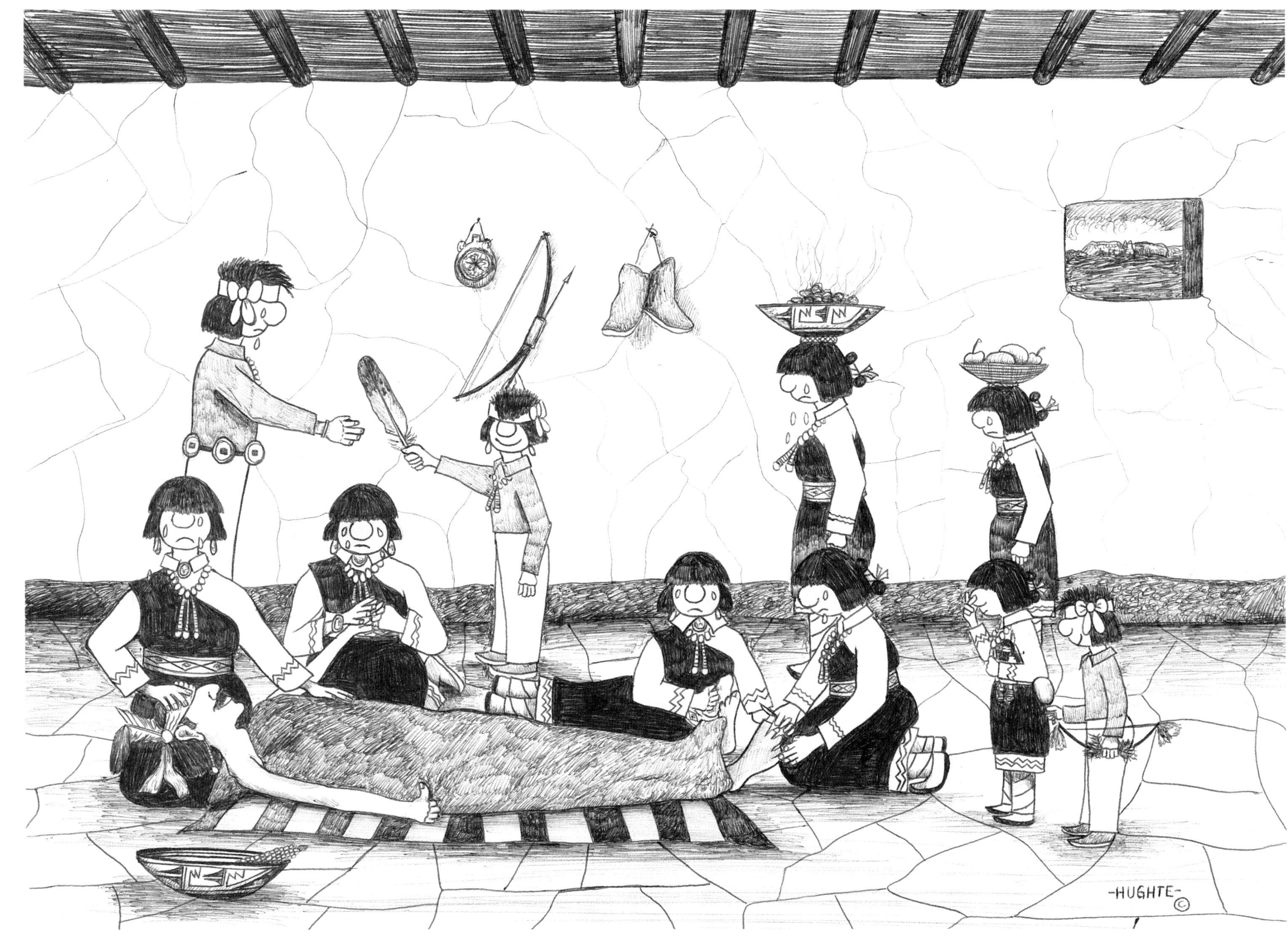
-HUGHTE- ©

Permit me to call your attention to the case of Mr. F. H. Cushing, your collector at Zuni Pueblo. Upon going among these people, instead of cooperating with the teachers of the school at that place, sustained jointly by the government and Presbyterian Church, he has persistently and unnecessarily thrown his influence against the school and, as we have reason to believe, pandered to the lowest passions of the people.

—Sheldon Jackson
[Presbyterian official]
letter to Spencer Baird,
December 22, 1882.

## No Bible, Please!

*Cushing was very protective of the Zunis and every time an outsider would come he would question them. Here some missionaries are visiting Zuni. The Zunis don't want anything to do with the White Man's religion or the Bible, so Cushing is telling the missionaries to go back where they came from.*

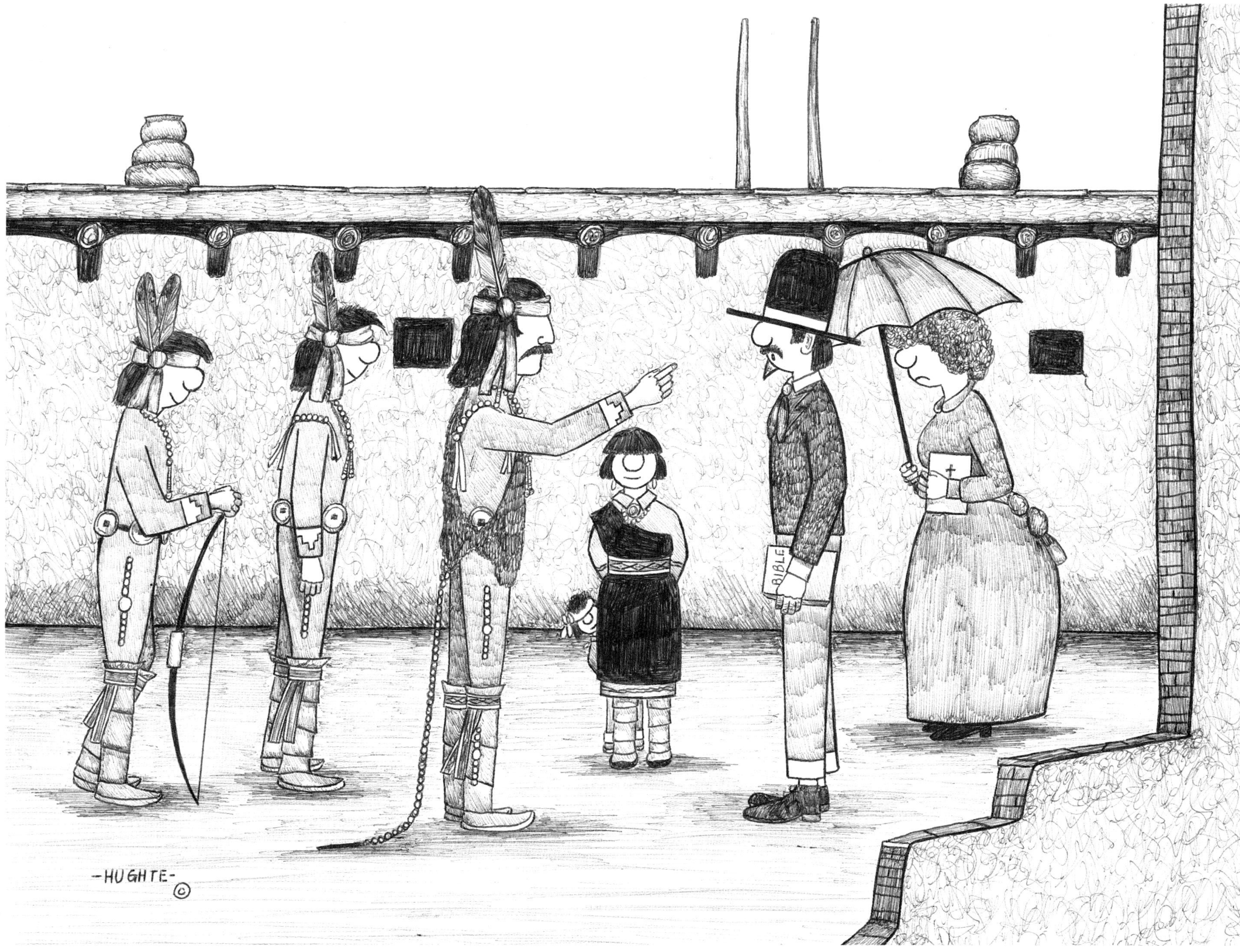
BIBLE
-HUGHTE- ©

## Off Limits

*Cushing is shooting at an innocent bystander—could be an Apache or Navajo, I don't know, I'd rather not say which—just an innocent bystander passing by Zuni land and Cushing shot his horse.*

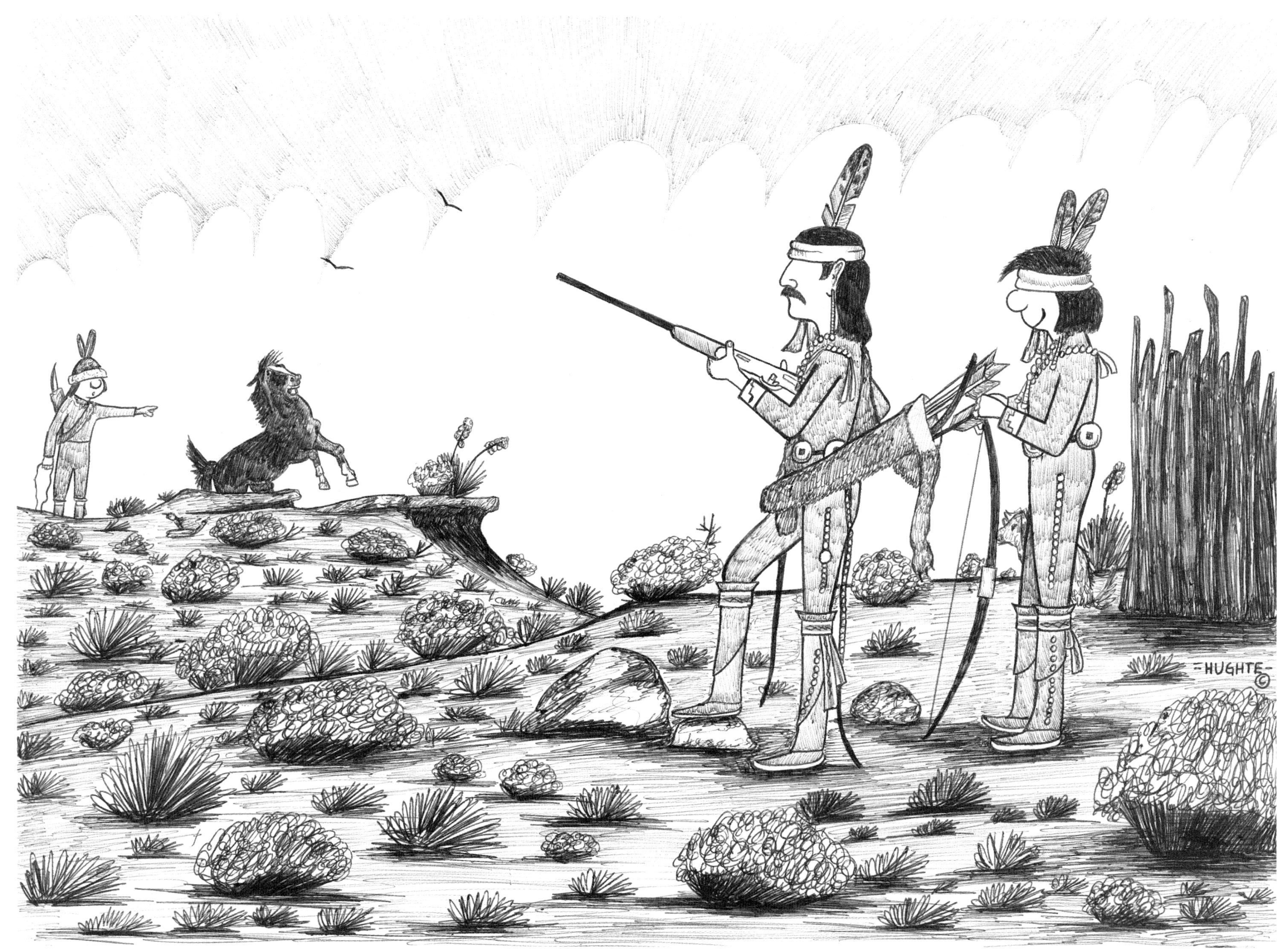
HUGHTE ©

# Cushing's Blind Date

*The Bow Priests are introducing Cushing to a Zuni lady because they were pushing him to marry a Zuni and to stay at the Pueblo rather than return to Washington.*

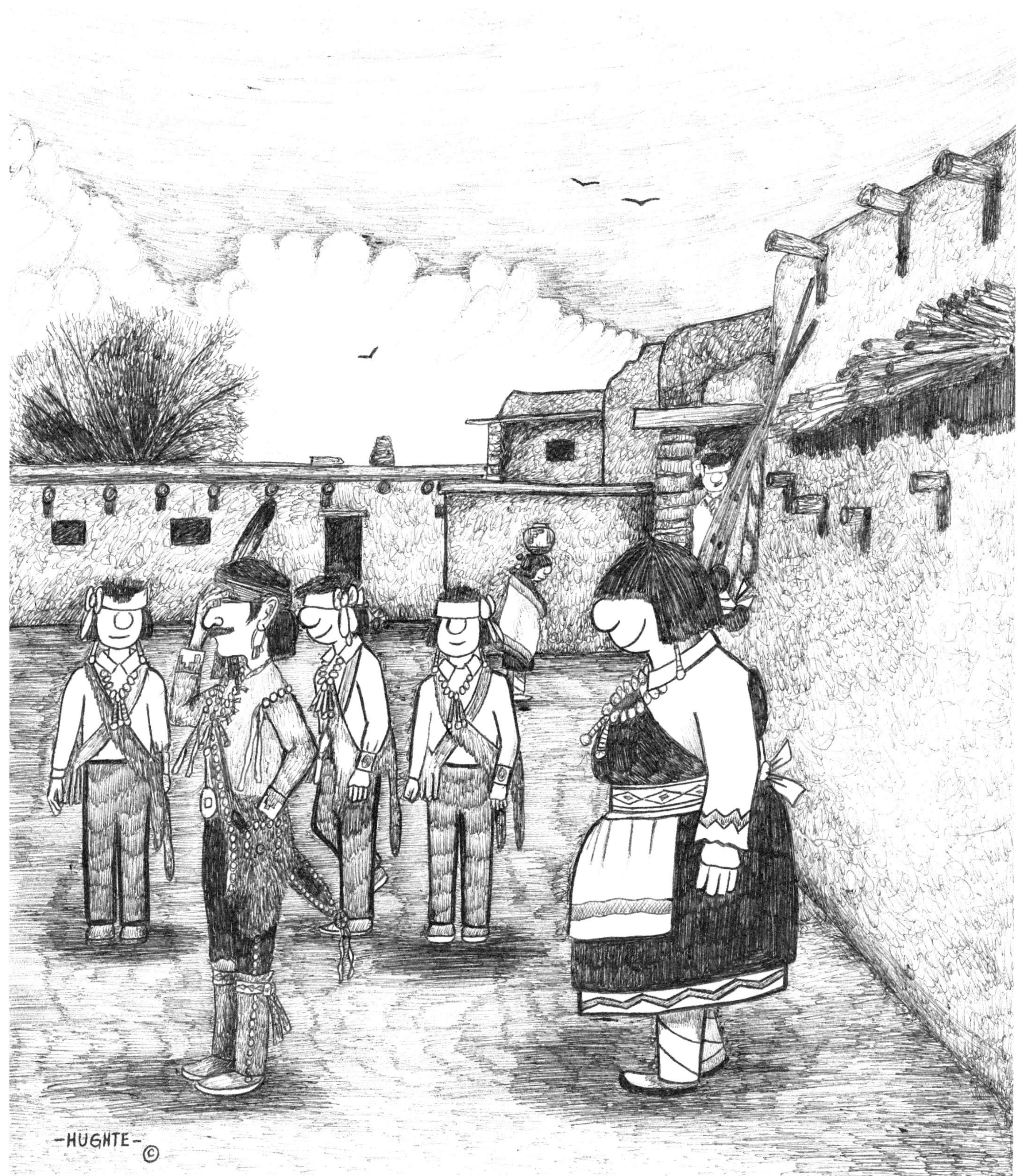
-HUGHTE-
©

# Going To Battle

*Cushing is about ready to go to war and here he is getting final messages from the Bow Priests. One Bow Priest is kind of playing, and is sticking an arrow in Cushing's buttocks.*

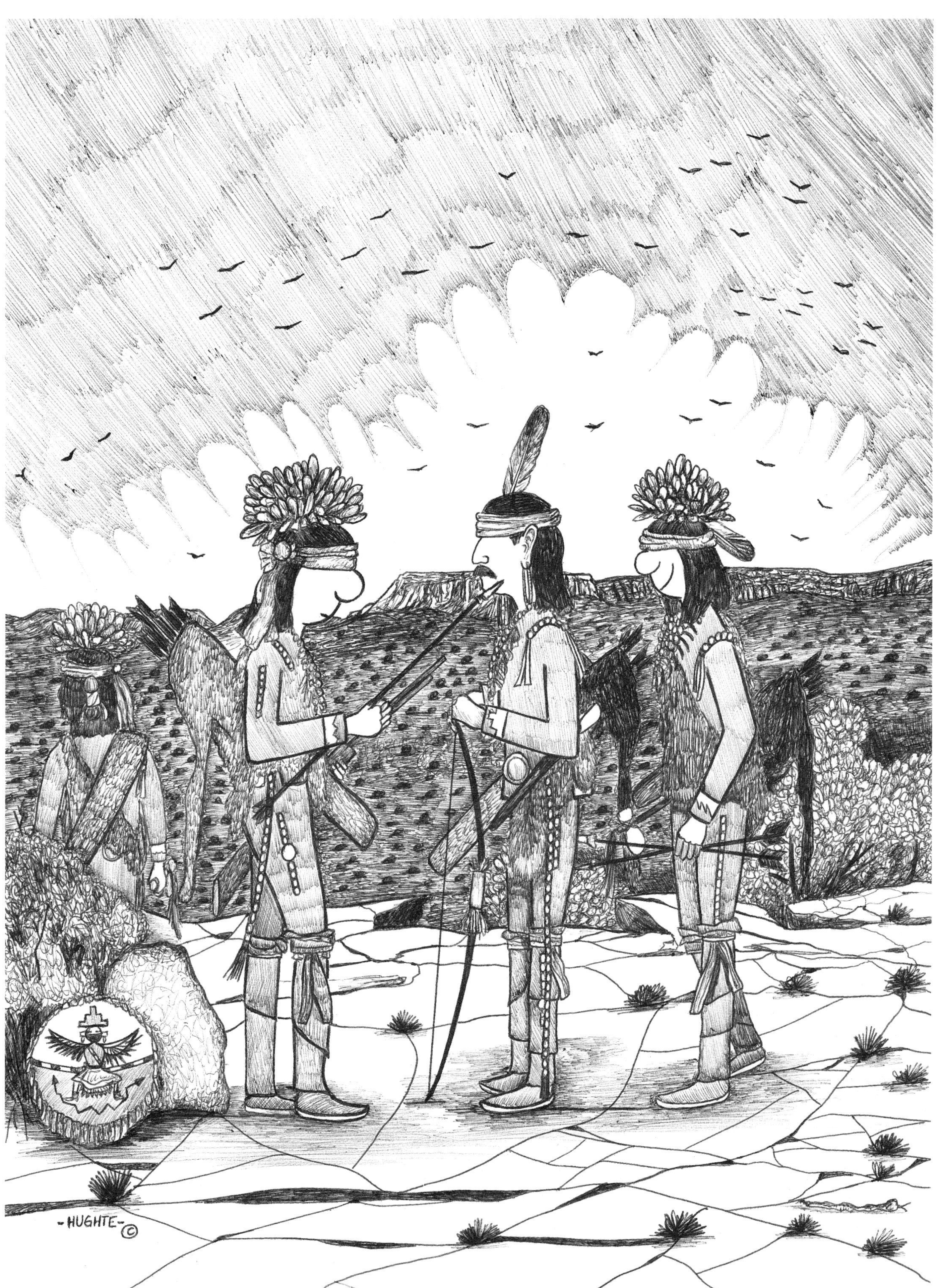
-HUGHTE- ©

The scalps procured for me by my father and officers of the Army were insufficient in themselves for [being admitted to the Bow Priesthood]; but the timely outbreak of the Apaches enabled me to acquire another and far more genuine article with right and title to possession . . .

—FHC letter to Sylvester Baxter, undated draft.

# Cushing's First Scalp

*I didn't want to show the individual getting scalped so what I did with this drawing is have Cushing coming up a hill with a scalp.*

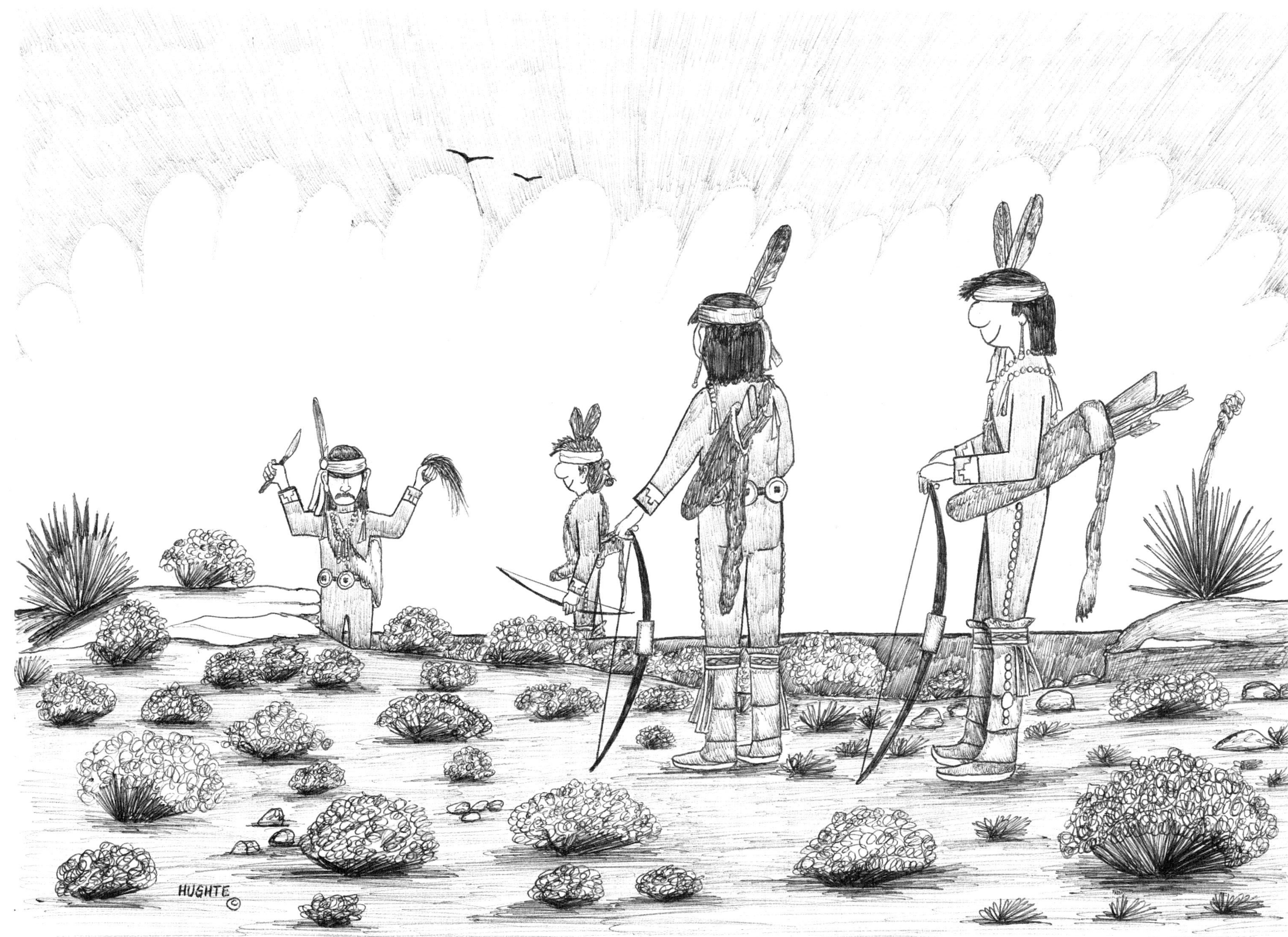
HUGHTE ©

## The Scalp Dance—

*After a scalping the Zunis have a Scalp Dance and here Cushing is taking part in a Scalp Dance.*

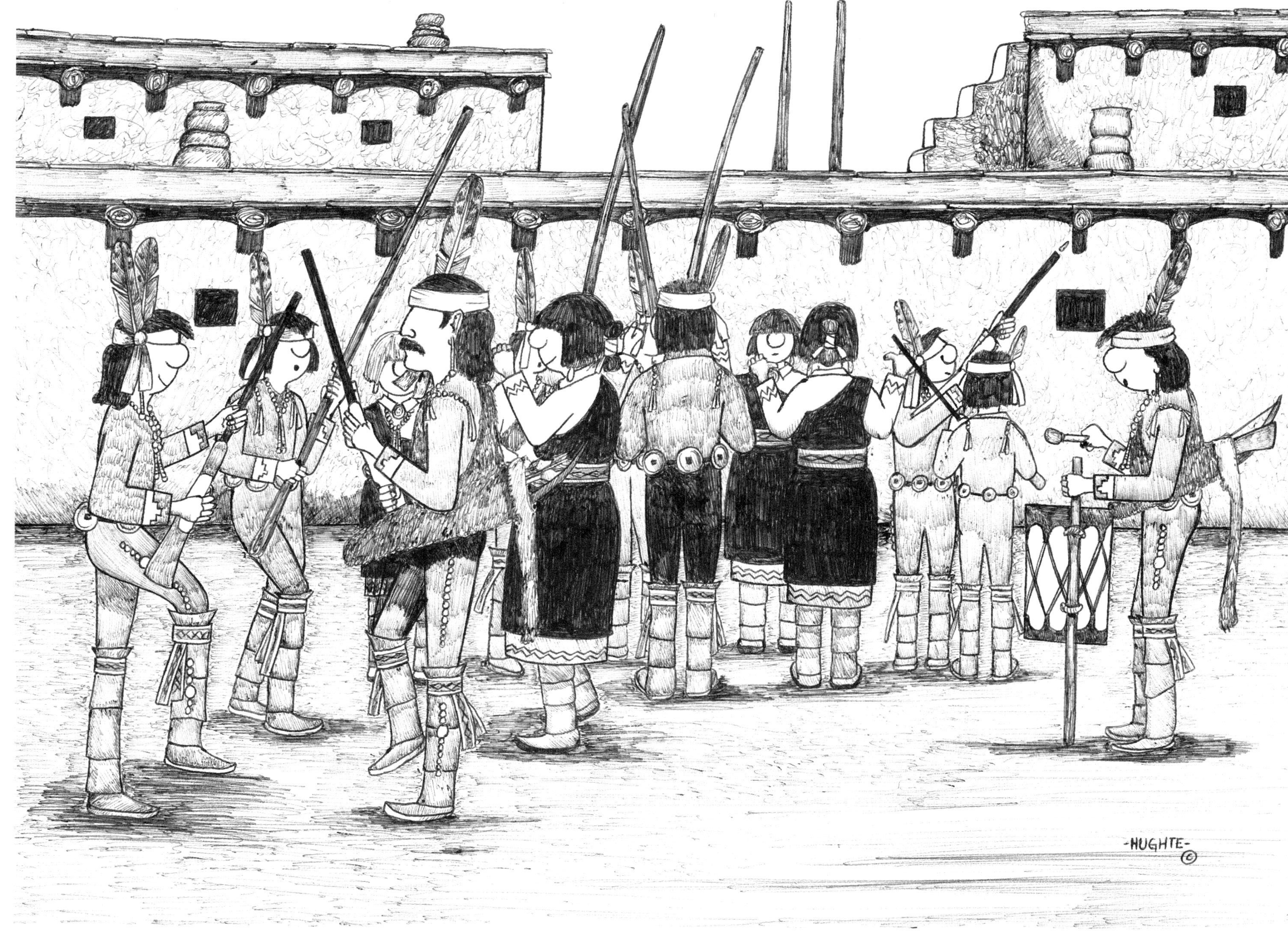
-HUGHTE-

# The Baptism

*What usually happens is that after a Scalp Dance the whole community gets washed to wash off the evil spirit. And here Cushing is getting himself washed.*

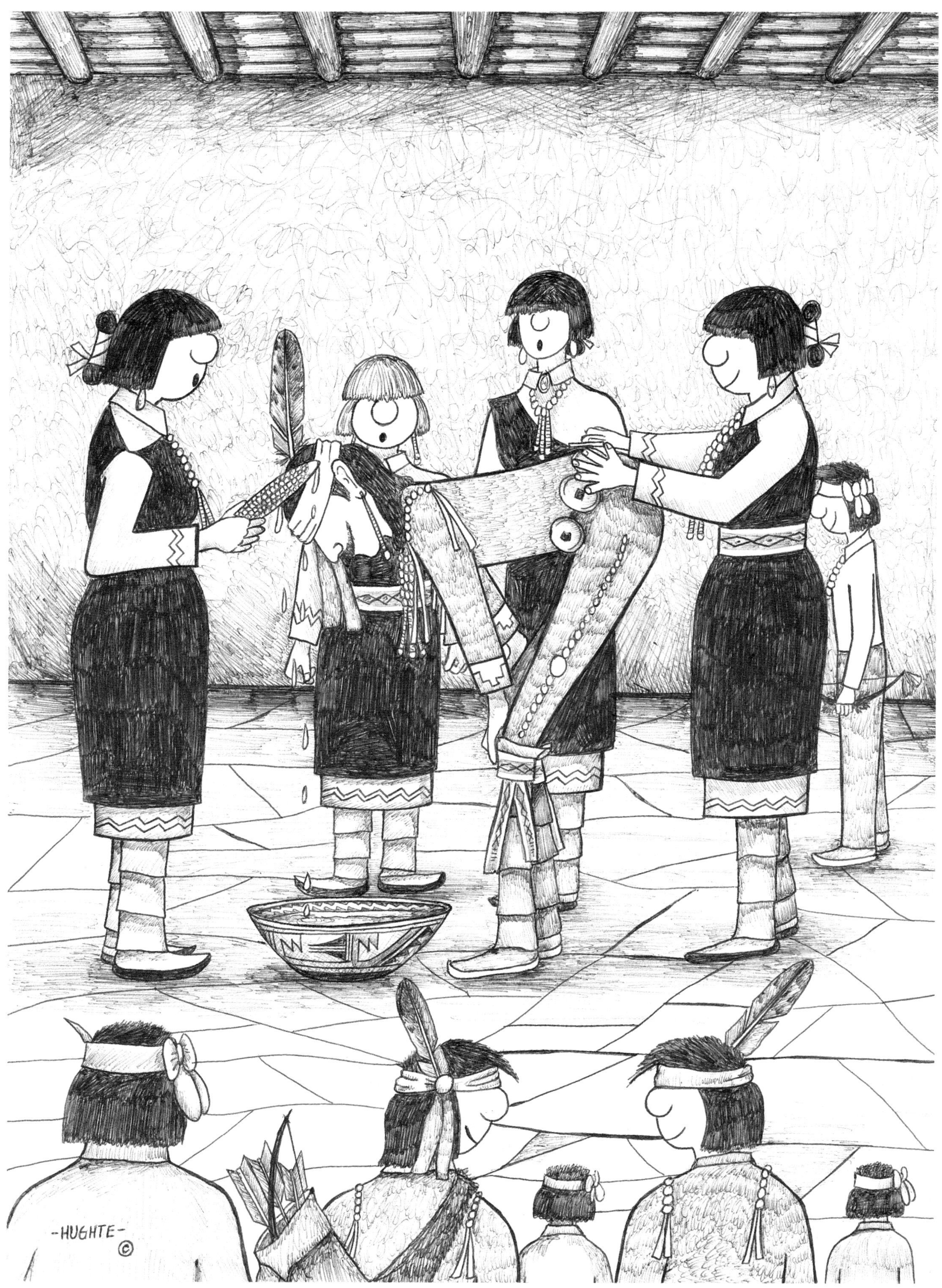
-HUGHTE-

The fine lot of imitation turquoises and corals sent me by Mr. Stevenson consisted simply of *three* of the former [one quarter inch in diameter], and of a quantity of wax beads, which though of interest at first, very nearly ruined my reputation when they came to melt upon their wearer's necks. . . .

—FHC letter to Spencer Baird,
March 12, 1881.

## Swap Meet

Cushing is *exchanging stuff from the East Coast for pottery. He is exchanging a kettle for a pot and then he also has garments that the Zuni ladies want. And that's what he is doing right now.*

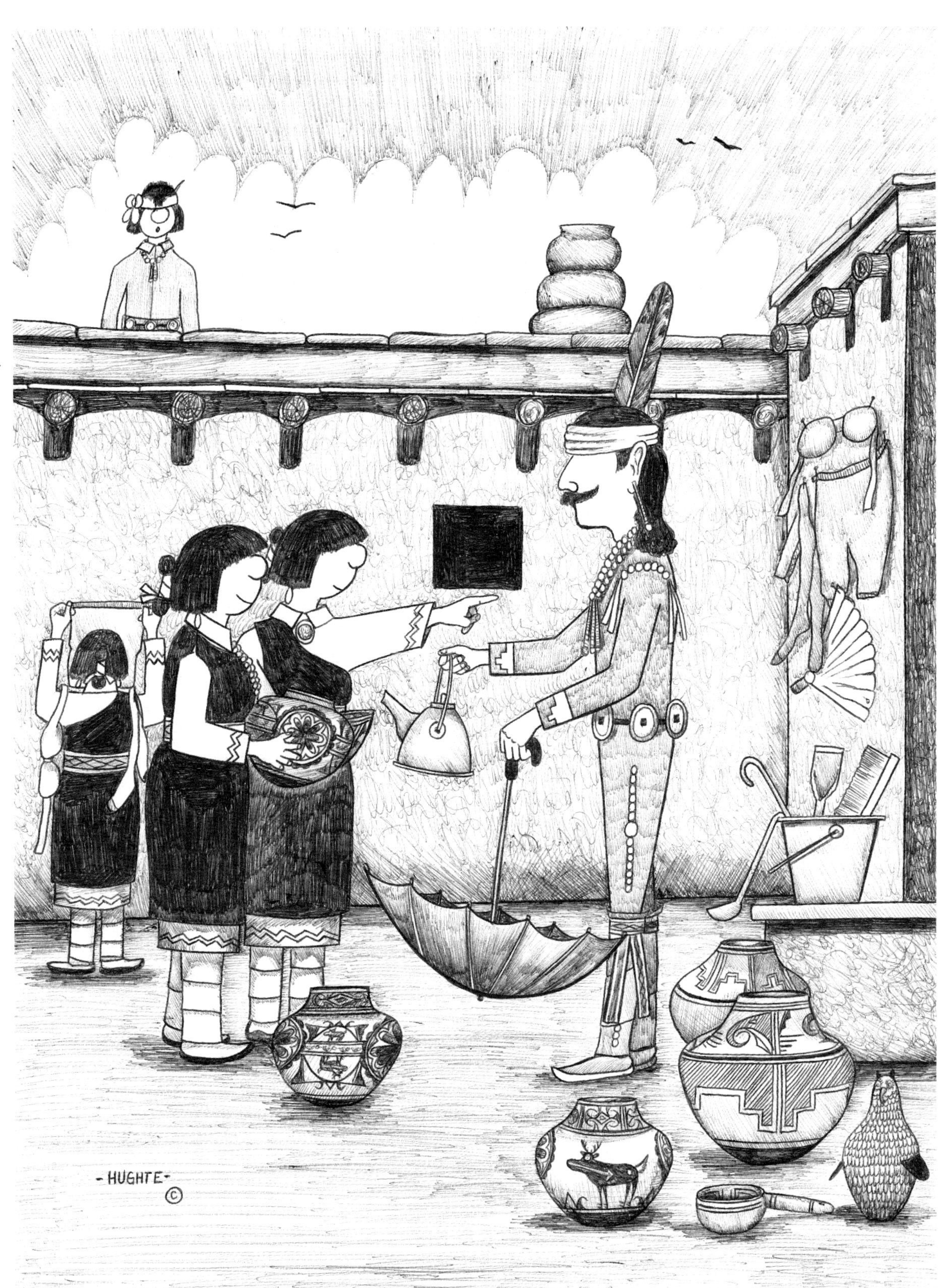
-HUGHTE-
©

# Making Prayer Sticks

*He has a little diagram on the wall on how to prepare a prayer stick. Notice the young Zunis are making fun of him.*

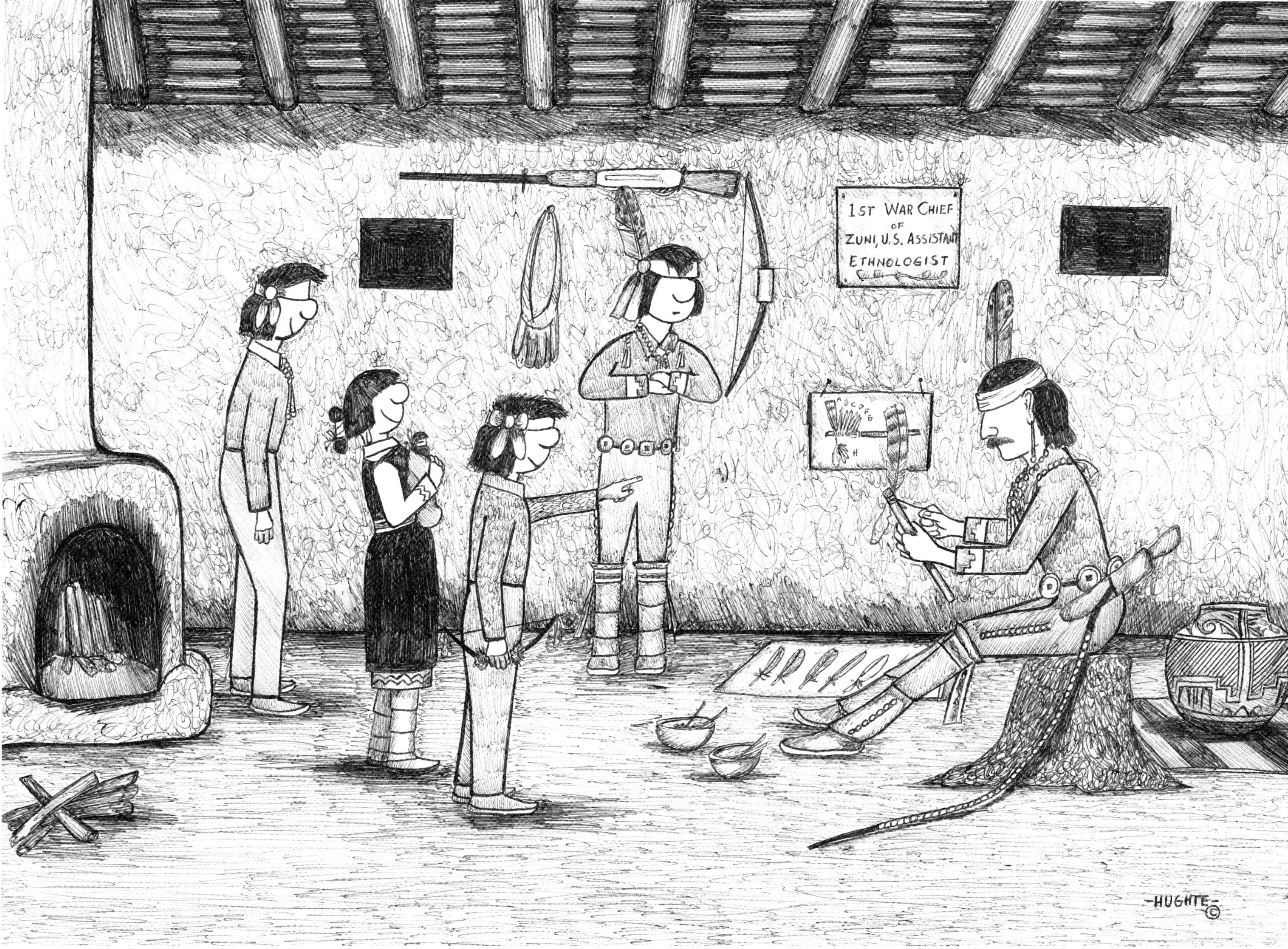
1ST WAR CHIEF
OF
ZUNI, U.S. ASSISTANT
ETHNOLOGIST
-HUGHTE-
©

# Off To D.C.

*He is on his way to Santa Fe to catch a train. And with all the swapping that he did—pottery and all—he has a wagonload of pottery and other Indian artifacts.*

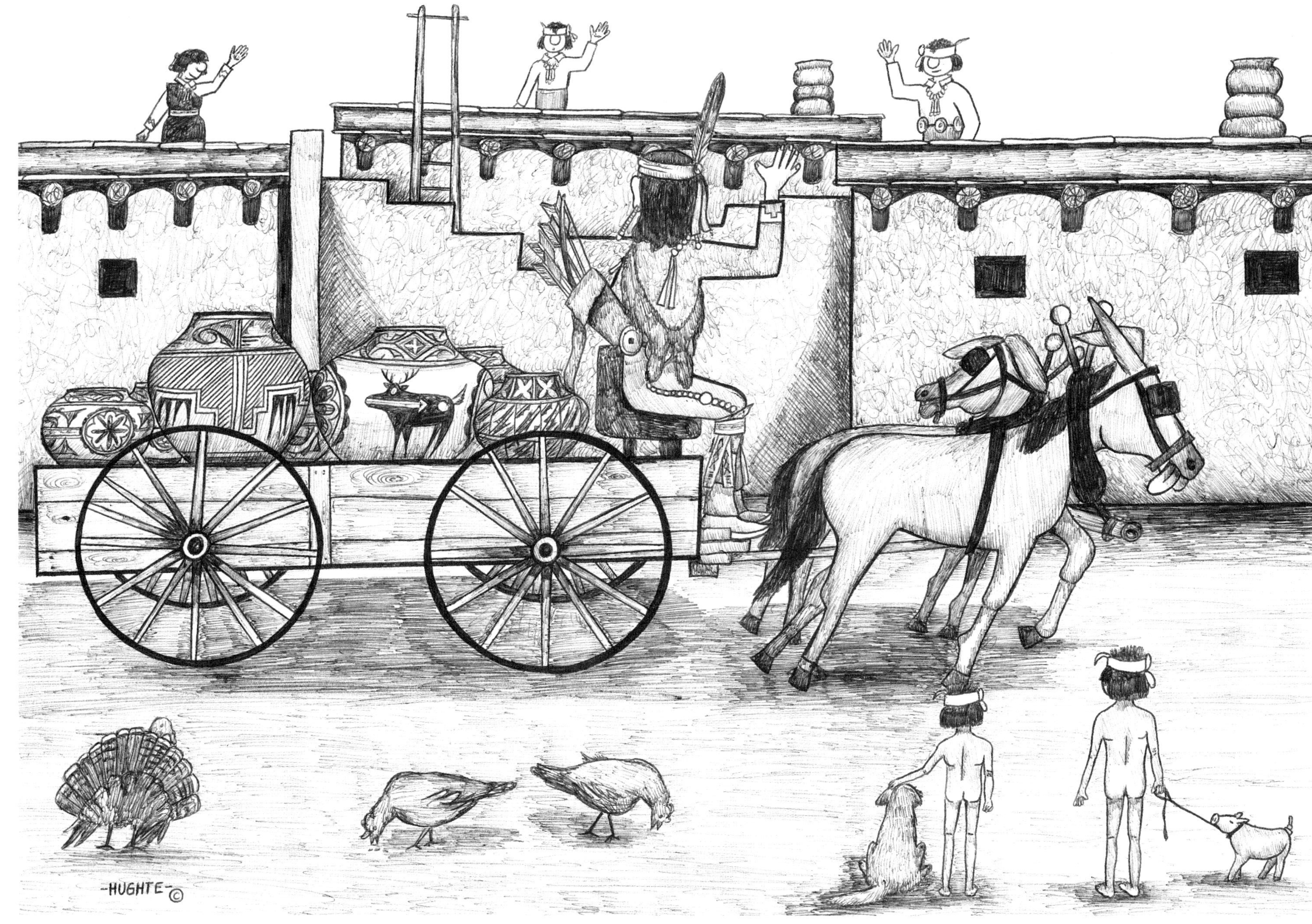
-HUGHTE-©

## Praying To The Locomotive

*Cushing took five Zunis to Washington, D.C. And here they are in Santa Fe about ready to go on board a locomotive, and the Zunis were so impressed with the engine that they decided to pray, so here the Zunis are praying to the locomotive.*

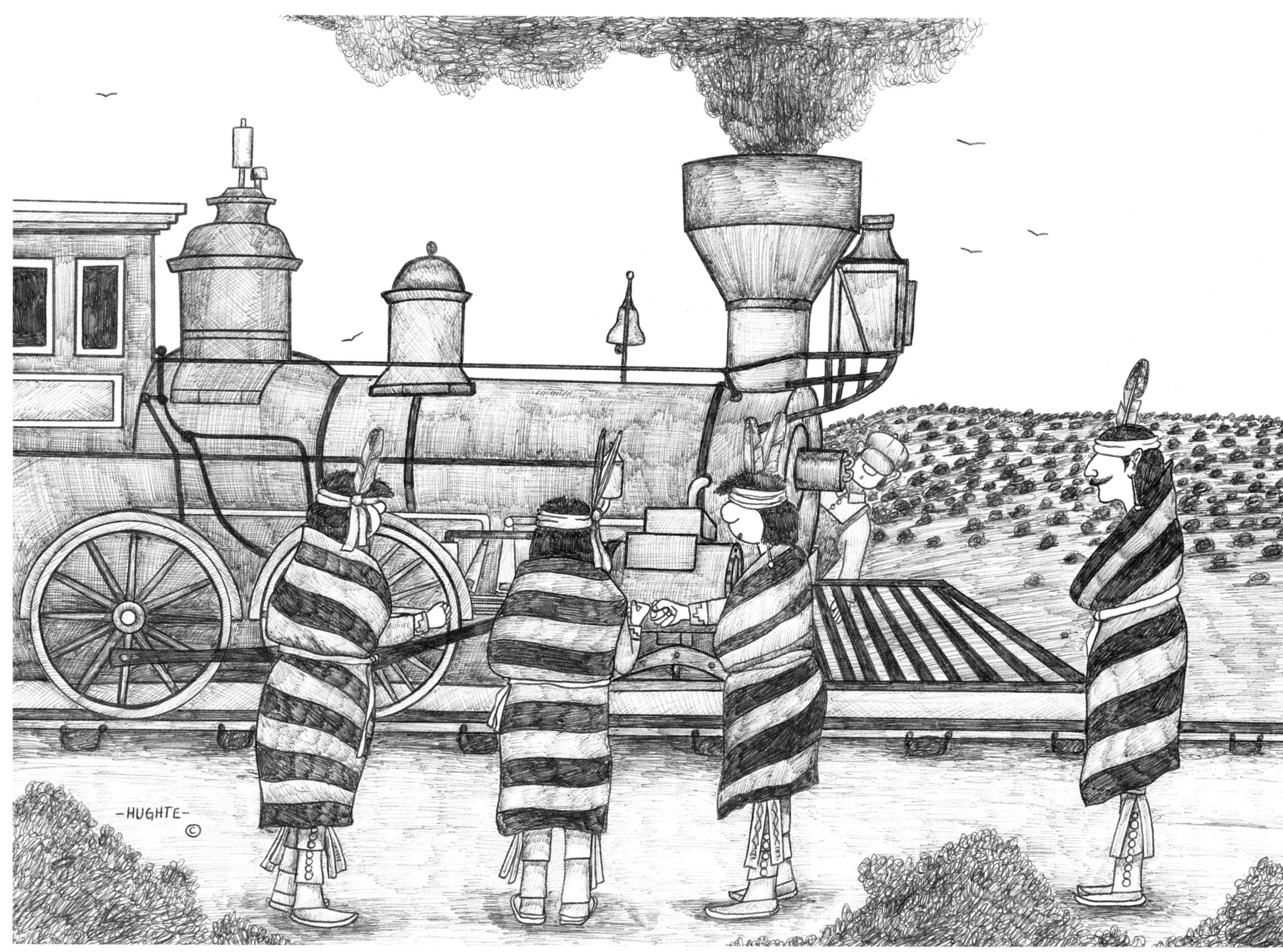
-HUGHTE-
©

# Five Zunis At The Capitol

*Cushing is showing the Zunis around Washington, D.C., and showing where the President of the United States works.*

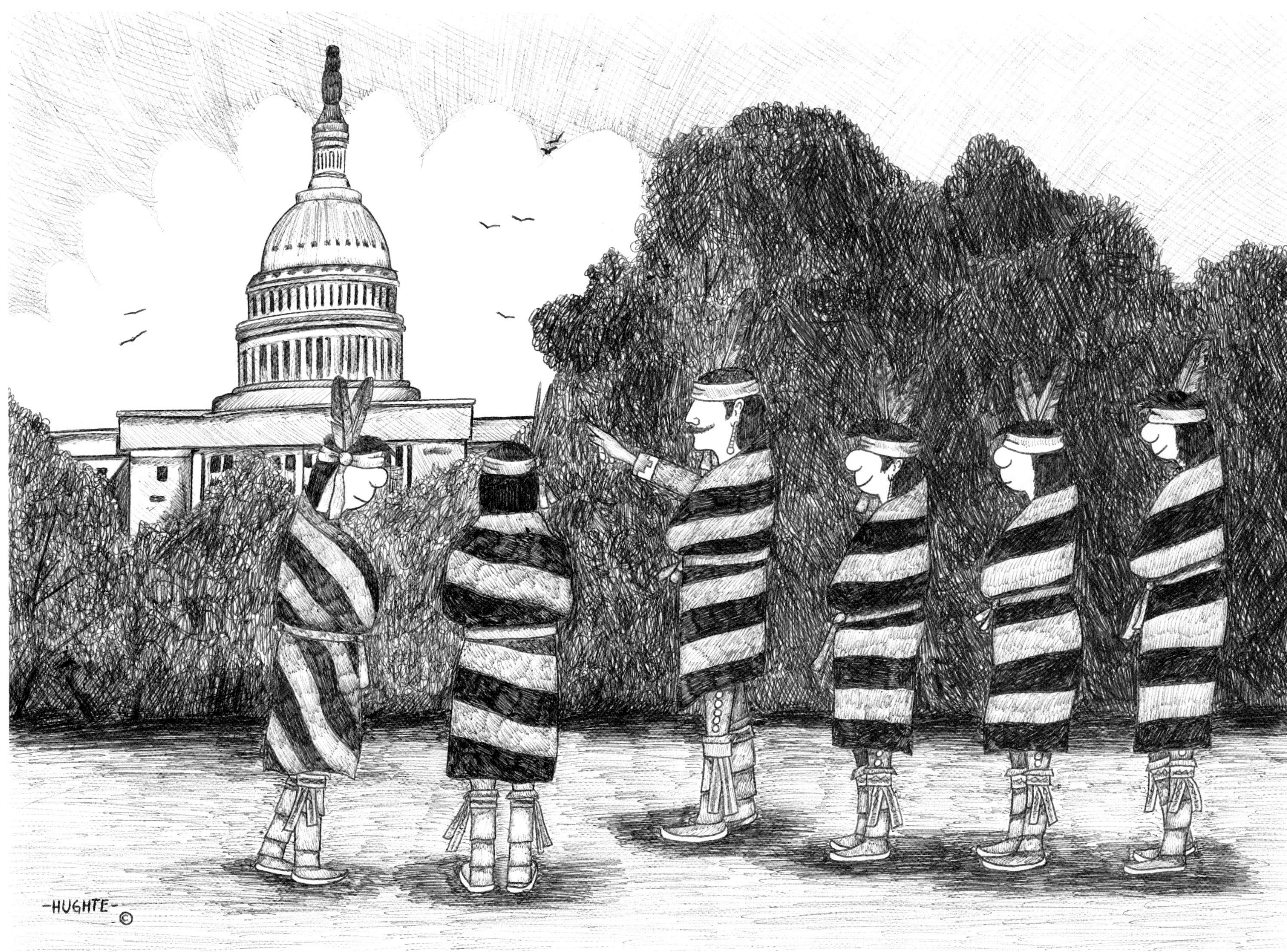
-HUGHTE- ©

Cushing has talents, but his appetite for notoriety alone would be enough to endanger his success.

—F. Parkman letter to Charles Norton, October 19, 1889.

# The Demo

*As he was on the East Coast he went to an all women's college and was doing a demonstration on pottery making.*

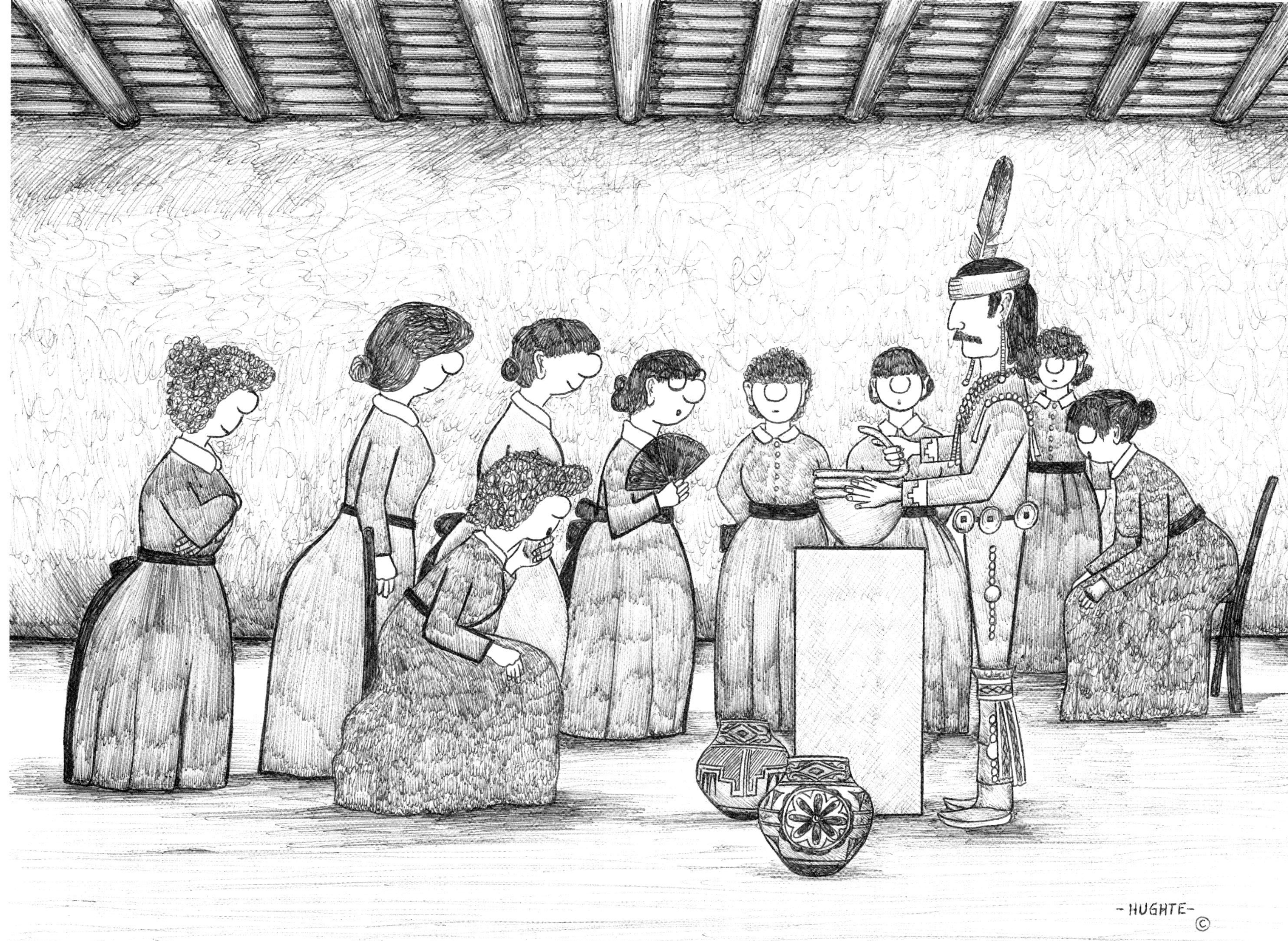
-HUGHTE-
©

# Zunis At Boston's Cheers—

*They are going to the Hampshire House to have dinner while the two Zunis are thinking about going down to Cheers.*

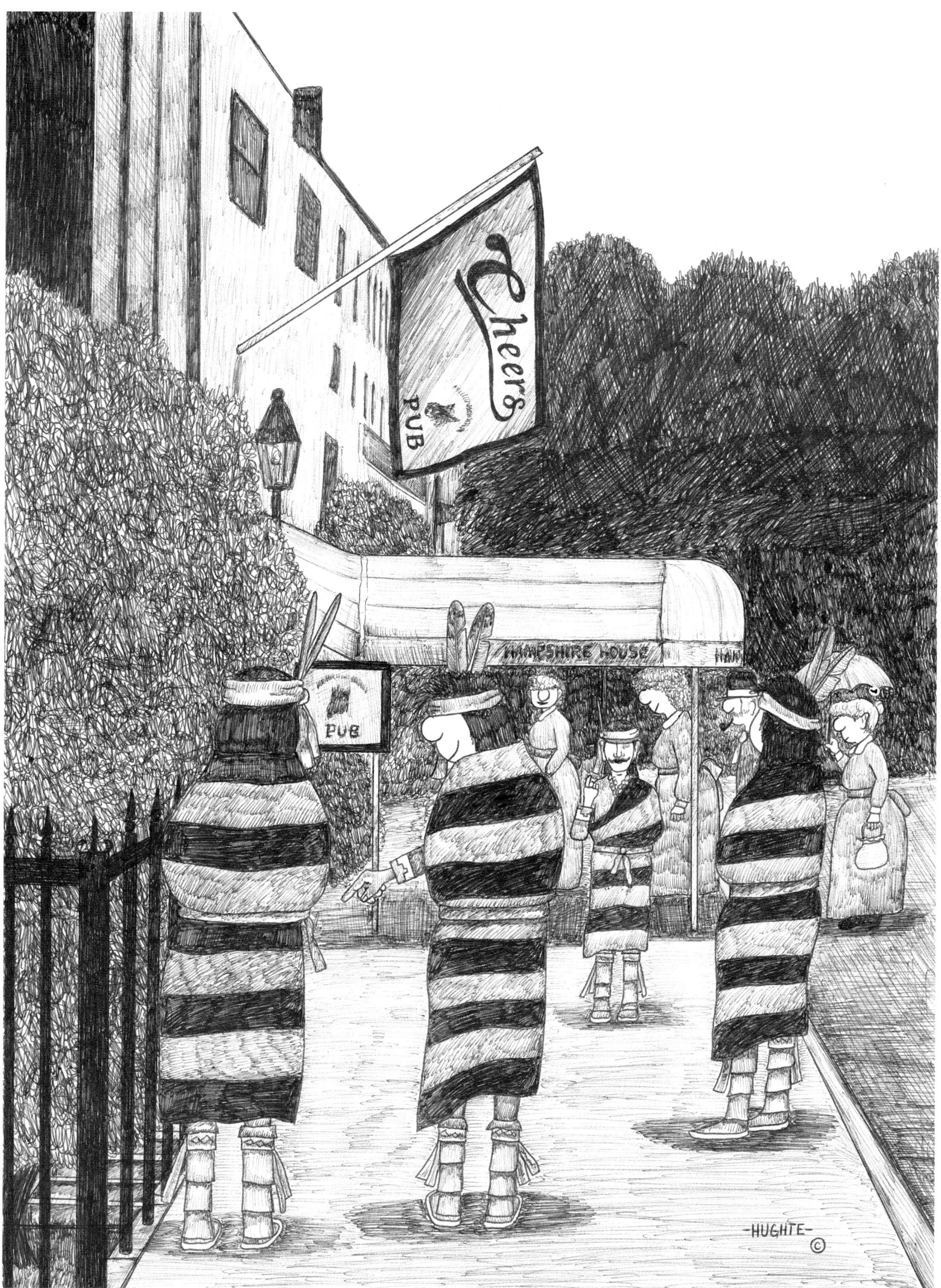
Cheers
PUB
HAMPSHIRE HOUSE
PUB
-HUGHTE-
©

# Dining At The Hampshire House—

*Here some Zunis are having lobster. Cushing is really all happy about eating lobster while the Zunis are wondering if they should eat it or not. One smart Zuni orders steak and Boston beans. Another Zuni gets up and decides he wants to have Boston beans and steak instead of lobster.*

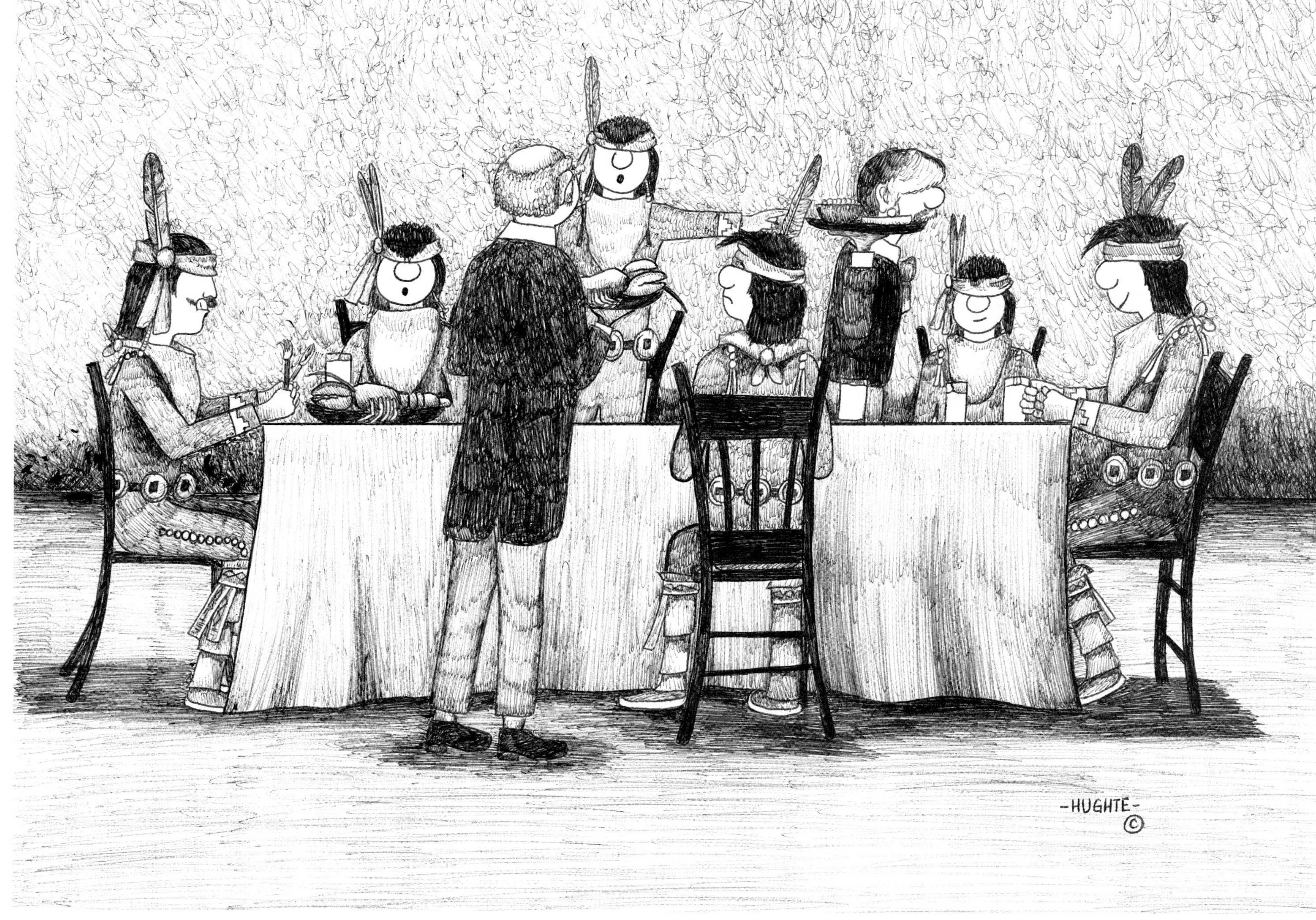
-HUGHTE-
©

The ocean ceremony was to be performed at Boston on account of the desire of the Zunis to get the water from as far to the eastward as possible and because of the interest felt in Mr. Cushing's work by his scientific friends there and in Cambridge. . . .

—Sylvester Baxter in
" An Aboriginal Pilgrimage,"
*Century Illustrated Monthly*
*Magazine* 1882.

# Collecting The Atlantic Water

*In the background is the U.S.S.* Constitution *sailing along. Cushing and his adopted father are observing the Zunis getting water.*

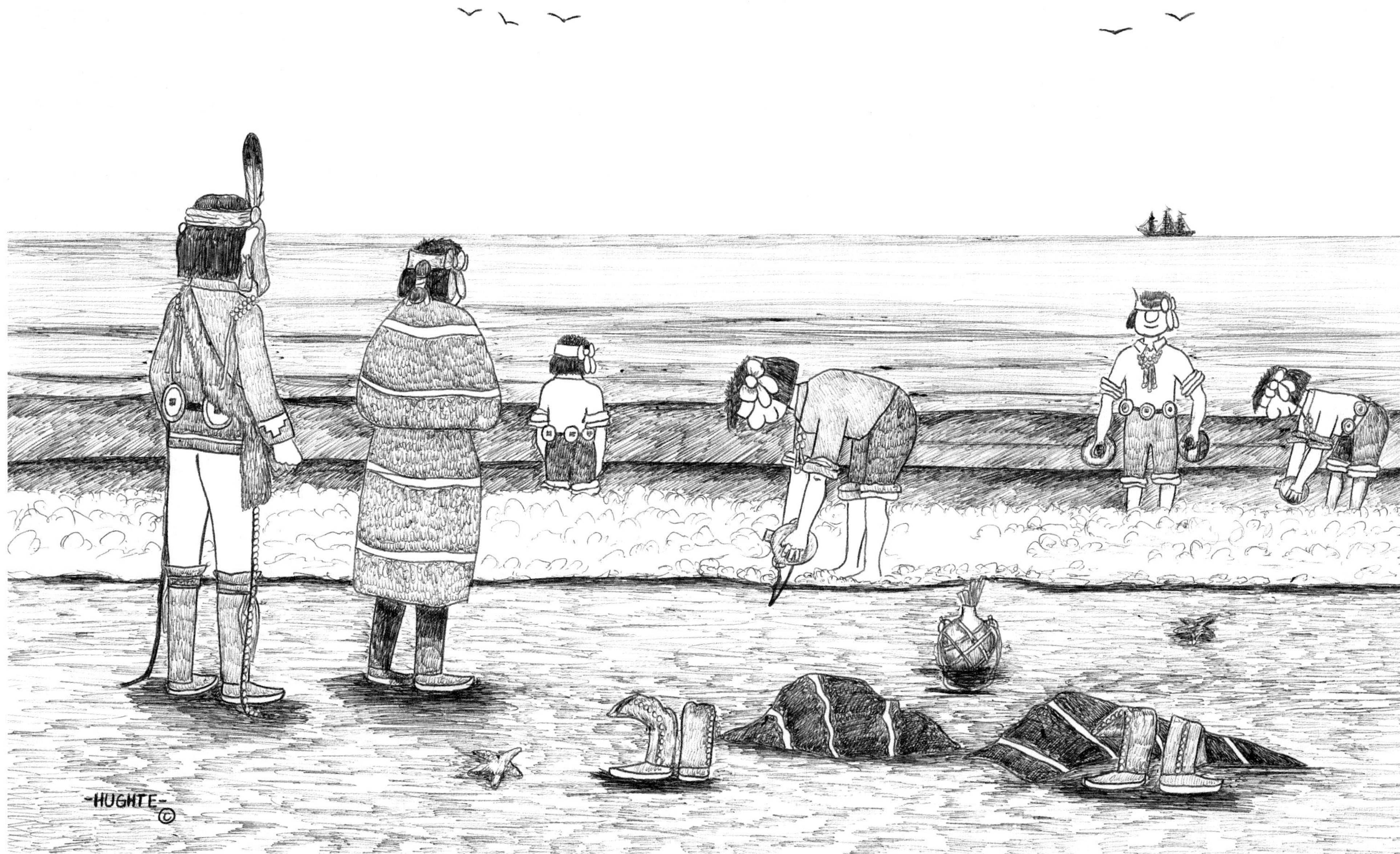
-HUGHTE- ©

# Cushing Getting Married To Emily —

*As he was on the East Coast he decided to get married. His Zuni buddies are watching him. One of them is crying, the rest are just watching. Three ladies are just admiring one young Zuni man instead of concentrating on the wedding.*

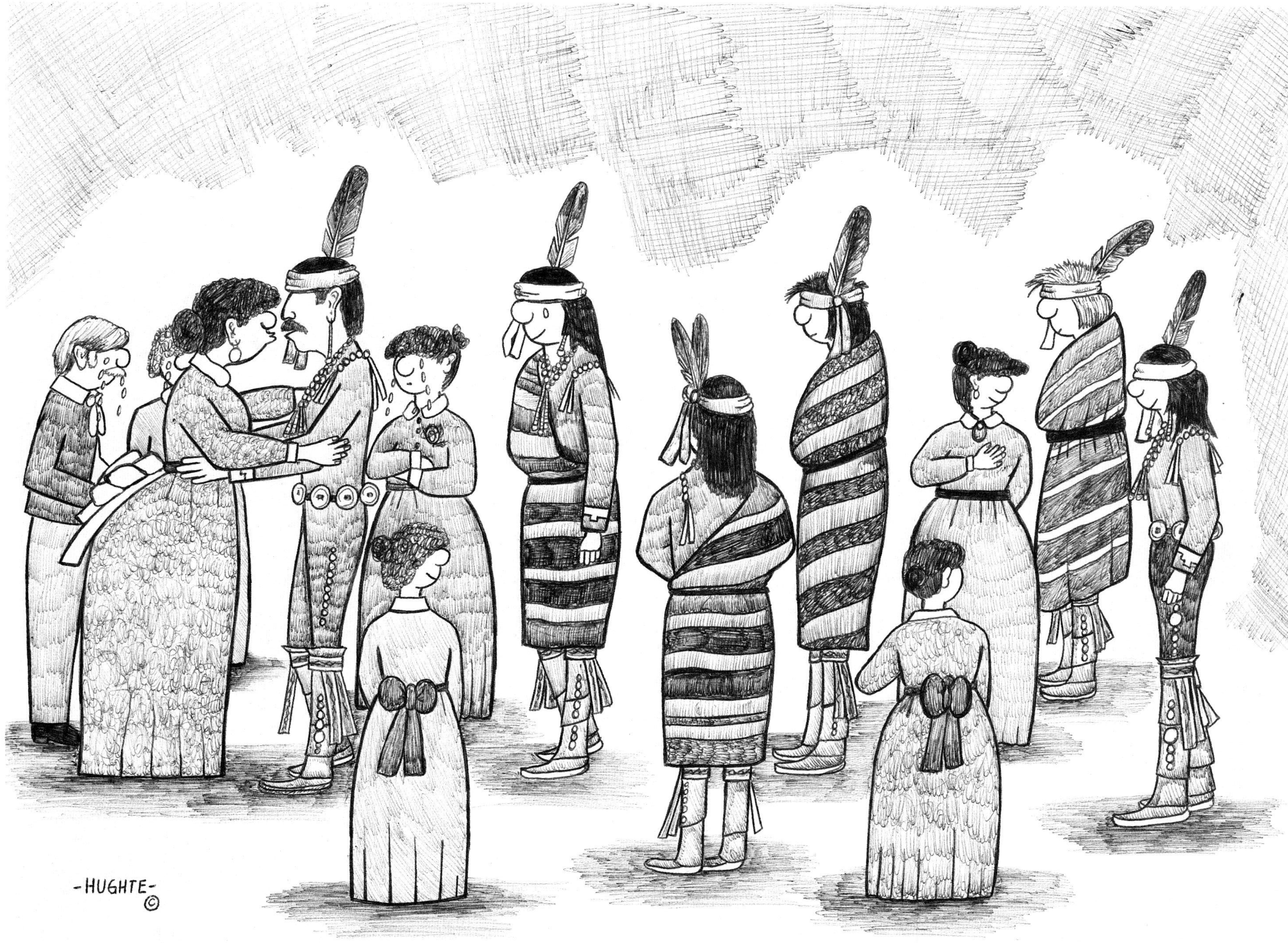
-HUGHTE-
©

Pretty soon there was a timid rap at the door—a custom Mrs. Cushing has introduced.

—William E. Curtis on "Mr. and Mrs. Cushing at Home," 1883.

# What You Should Do When You Go To Cushing's House

*Cushing brought his wife to Zuni and they lived somewhere near Halona Plaza. Two Zunis are just walking into Cushing's home when Cushing and Emily are making love. Emily gets so upset because she has no privacy and goes out steaming mad and tells the two Zunis, "This is our way. You come to our house and you knock on the door!" So this illustration tells you what you should do when you go to Cushing's house.*

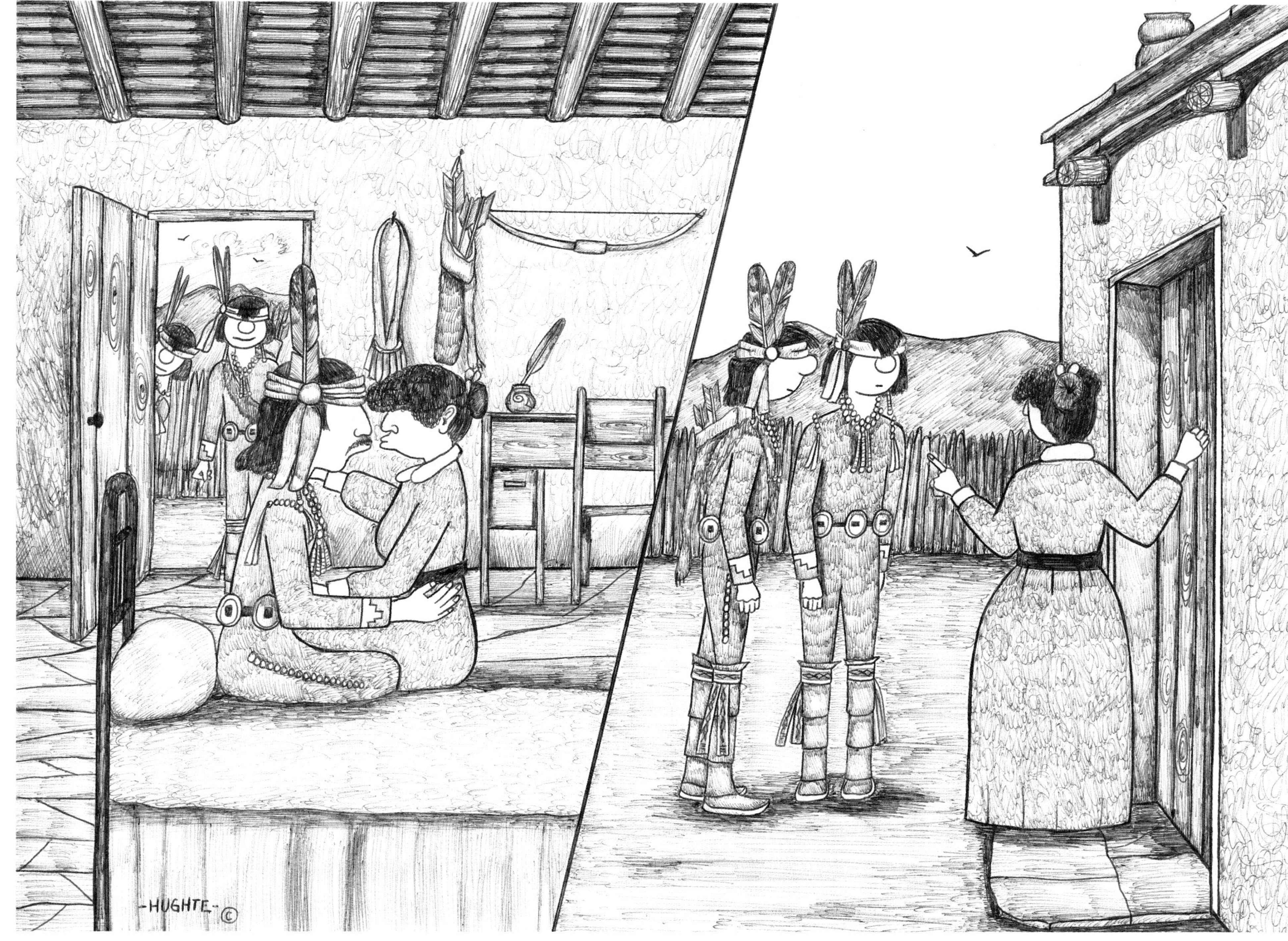
-HUGHTE-©

# Making Emily Jealous

*Two Zuni ladies are trying to make Emily jealous. They are kind of testing her to see what type of person she is, to see if she is a jealous person or not. An old lady is just smiling away working on her pottery.*

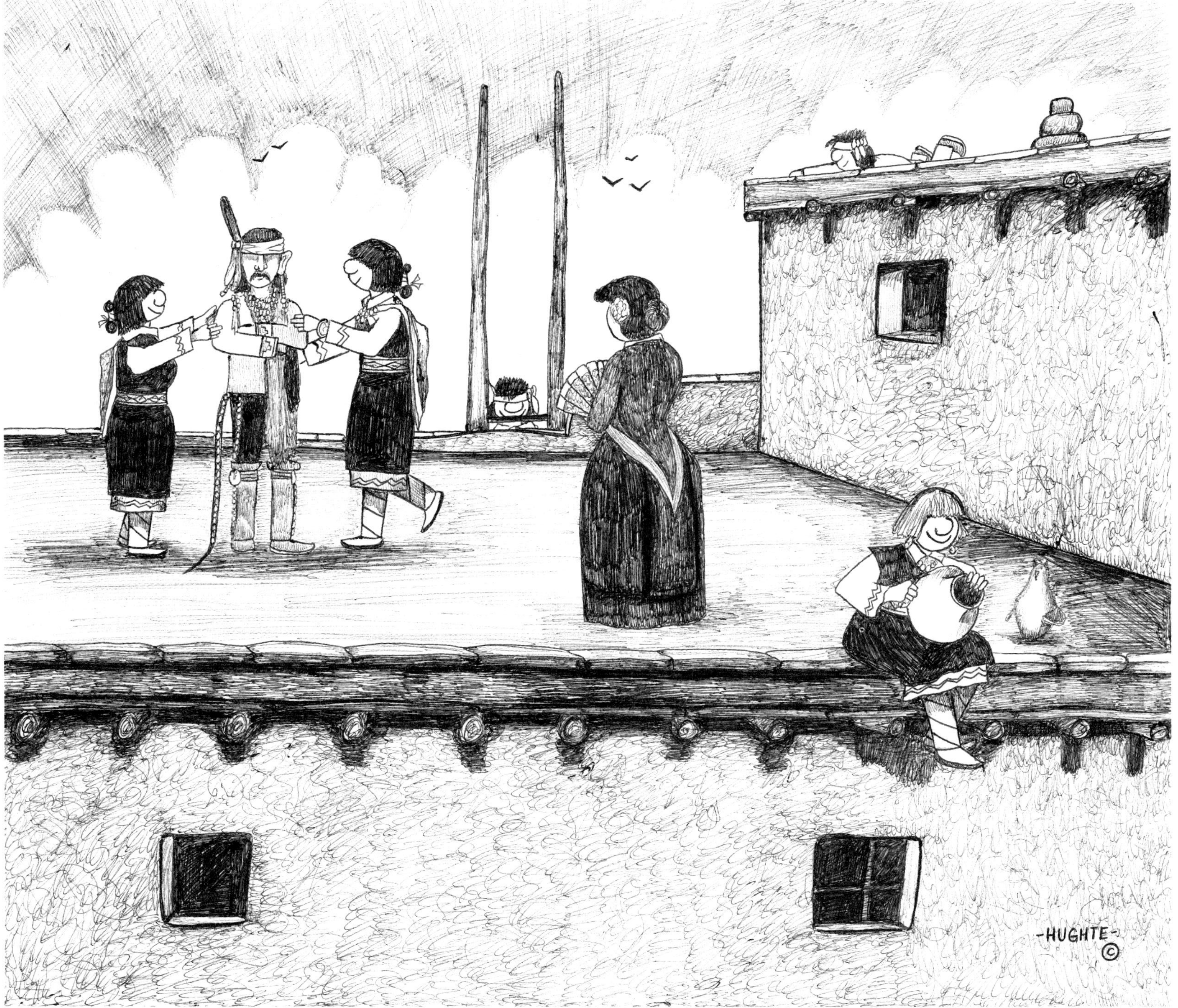
-HUGHTE- ©

# Off To Hopi

*Everybody is waving them goodbye and they were so happy to leave they forgot to untie their dog. The dog is being dragged while everybody is waving except for the two kids pointing and trying to get Cushing's attention that his dog is tied up.*

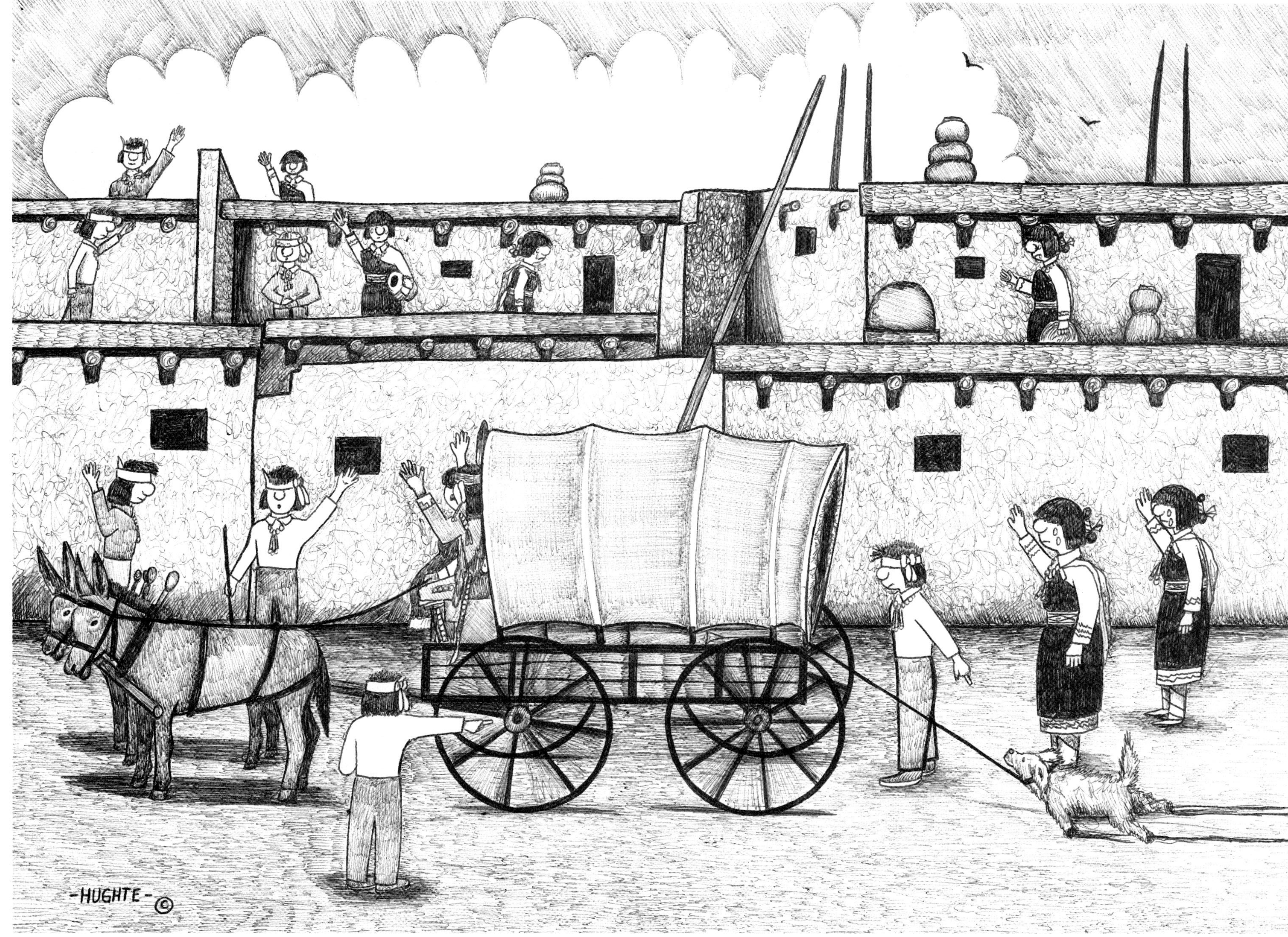
-HUGHTE- ©

# Zuni Land, Bucko!—

*Cushing is arguing with two soldiers that Senator Logan sent. The soldiers wanted to make an 800-acre ranch and Cushing is telling them that this is Zuni land. One of the soldiers was Logan's son-in-law—so that became a heated argument. So here is Cushing protecting the Nutria area.*

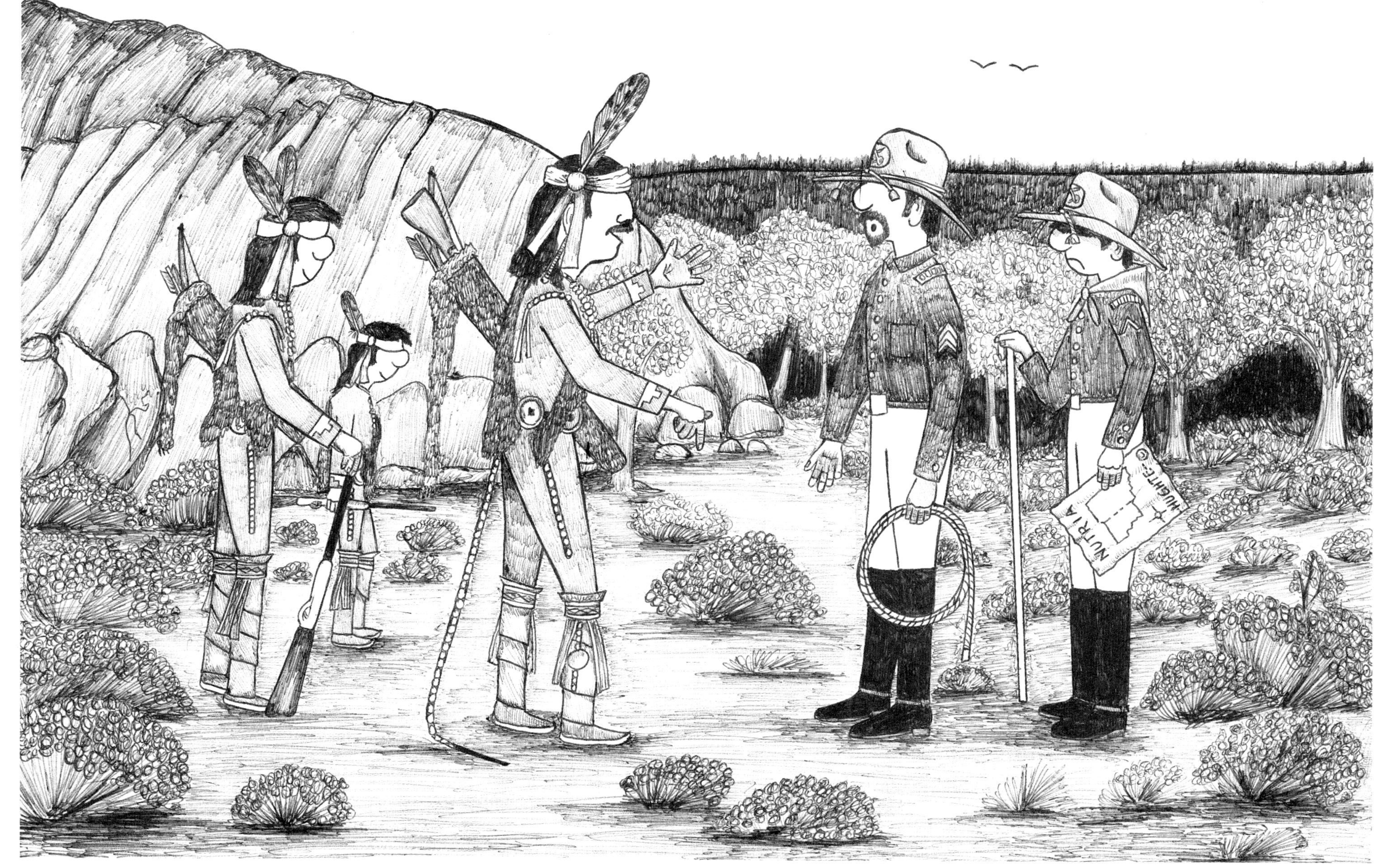
NUTRIA
HUGHTE

Dear Sir:

I beg to call your attention to that clause of your letter of instructions in which you are directed to submit to this office monthly reports of your operations, and I request that said instructions be complied with.

No reports have been received from you since your return to Zuni—about the first of September last.

By order of the Director:

Very truly yours,
James C. Pilling
Chief Clerk

—Pilling letter to FHC,
January 30, 1883.

# Yes, I Can Take A Picture!

*Cushing is telling Matilda Coxe Stevenson not to take photographs of the Kachinas, but Matilda was so stubborn that she had to have everything her way. Here she takes her umbrella and hits him over the head while the little Kachina Dancer is wondering what the heck this box is and is shaking his rattle at the camera.*

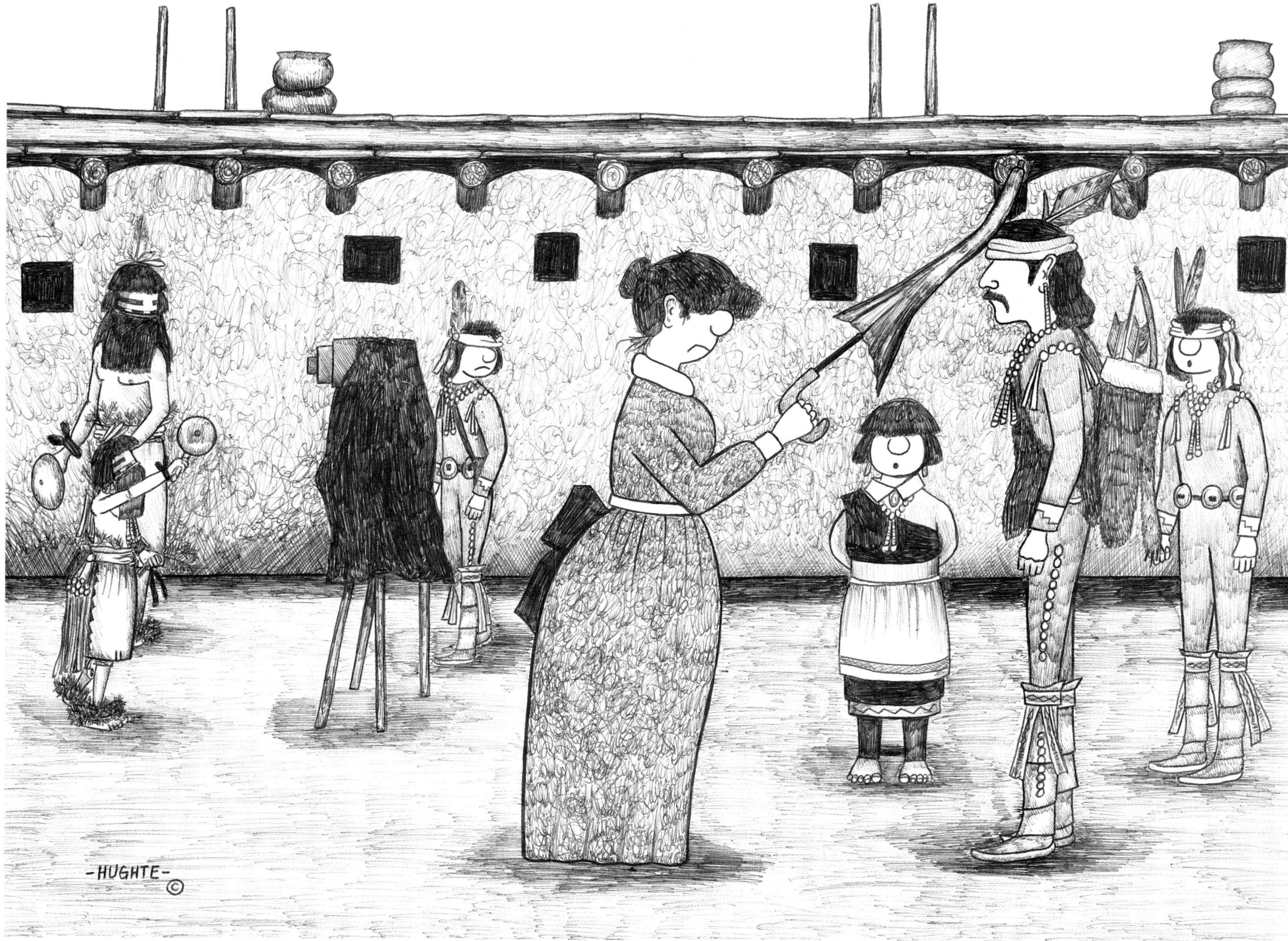
-HUGHTE- ©

Frank Hamilton Cushing in his fantastic dress worn while among the Zuni Indians. This man was the biggest fool and charlatan I ever knew. He even put his hair up in curl papers every night. How could a man walk weighed down with so much toggery?

—Written comment by Matilda Coxe Stevenson on back of photograph among the Cushing Papers at the Southwest Museum.

## The Big Photo

*Here Cushing is getting his portrait done. This is just an artist's perception of what I thought it might have looked like. And here, of course, are some Zuni kids making fun of him, and two Zuni ladies just admiring him the way he is standing.*

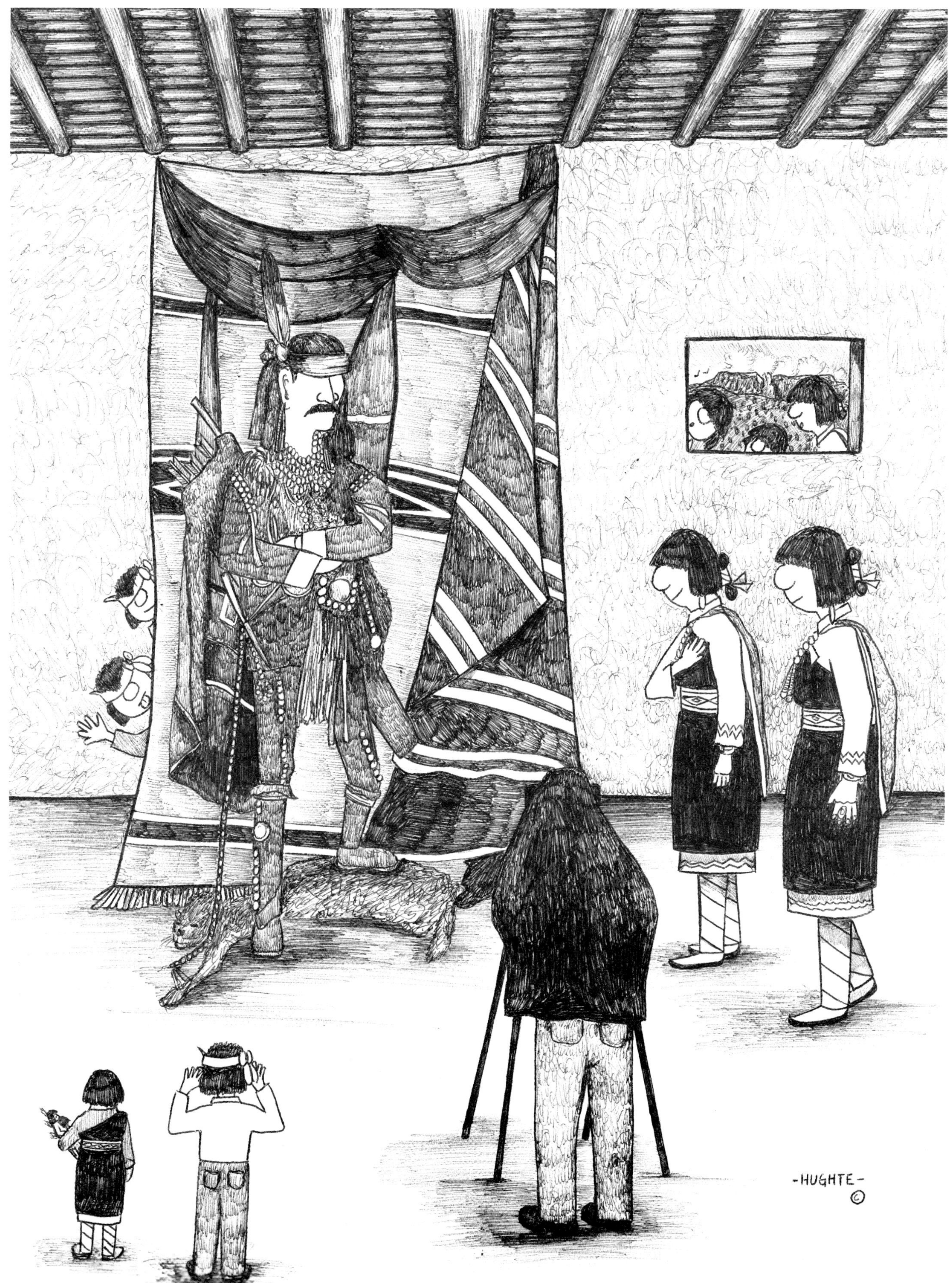
-HUGHTE-
©

# Bad Boy Cushing —

*This is one drawing I will never forget. This drawing got me really upset and depressed that someone who is so helpful and loyal to the Zuni people would go back to the Smithsonian and do such a terrible thing. Here Cushing creates a Mudhead mask. On the right you can see a sewing machine and he is using paint and scissors and canvas on the floor while people are taking photographs of him. This was a very uncomfortable drawing for me to do.*

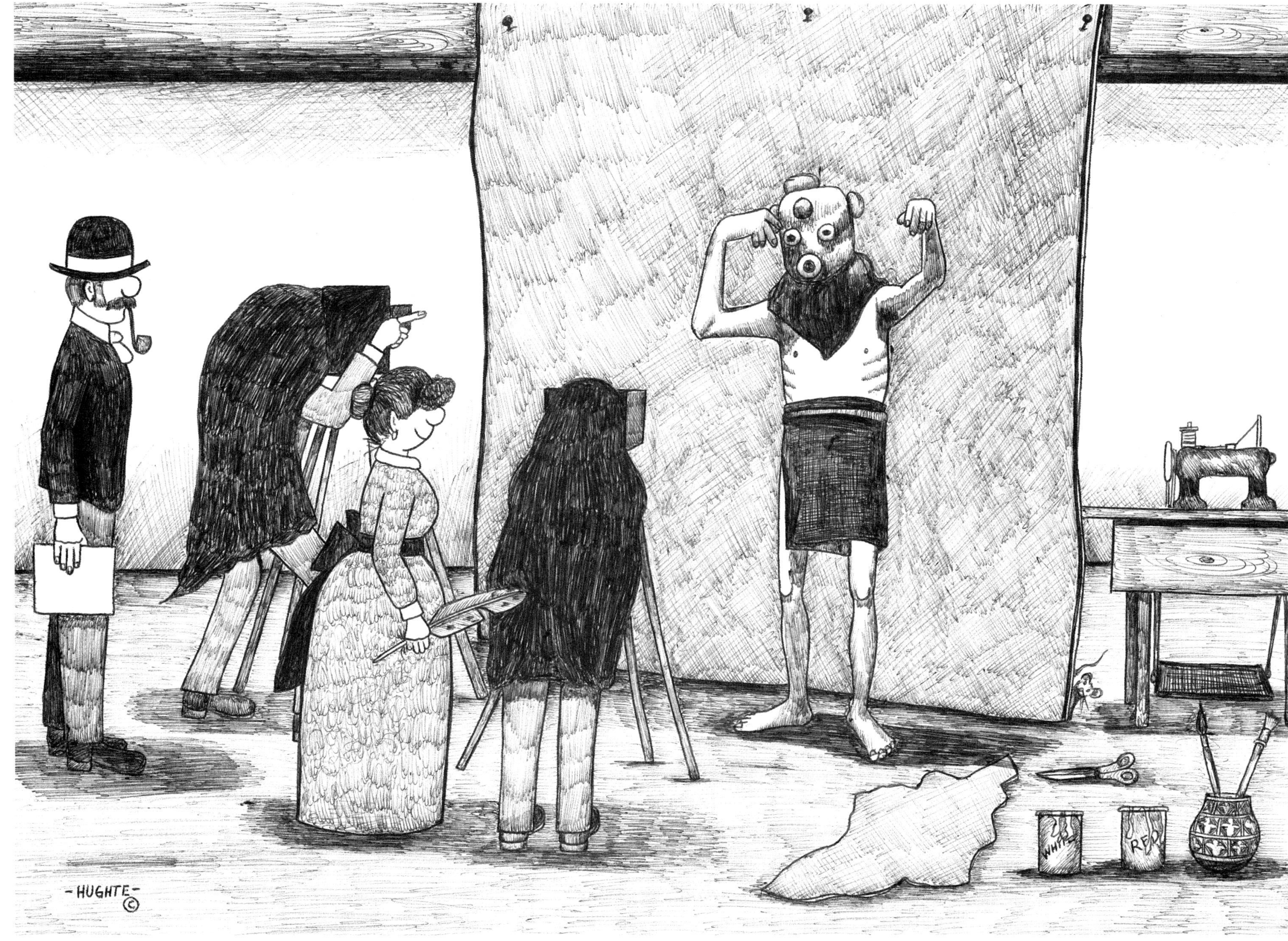
RED
-HUGHTE-
©

# My Punishment

*There are four Zunis who want to punish him in four different ways. The White Lady brought the photo to the head Kachina Priest and the elderly Zuni lady is crying away. The first Zuni wants to cut his head off; the second Zuni would like to hang him; the third to castrate him, and the fourth Zuni would like to initiate him. And there is a little kid being dragged away because he is not initiated at all.*

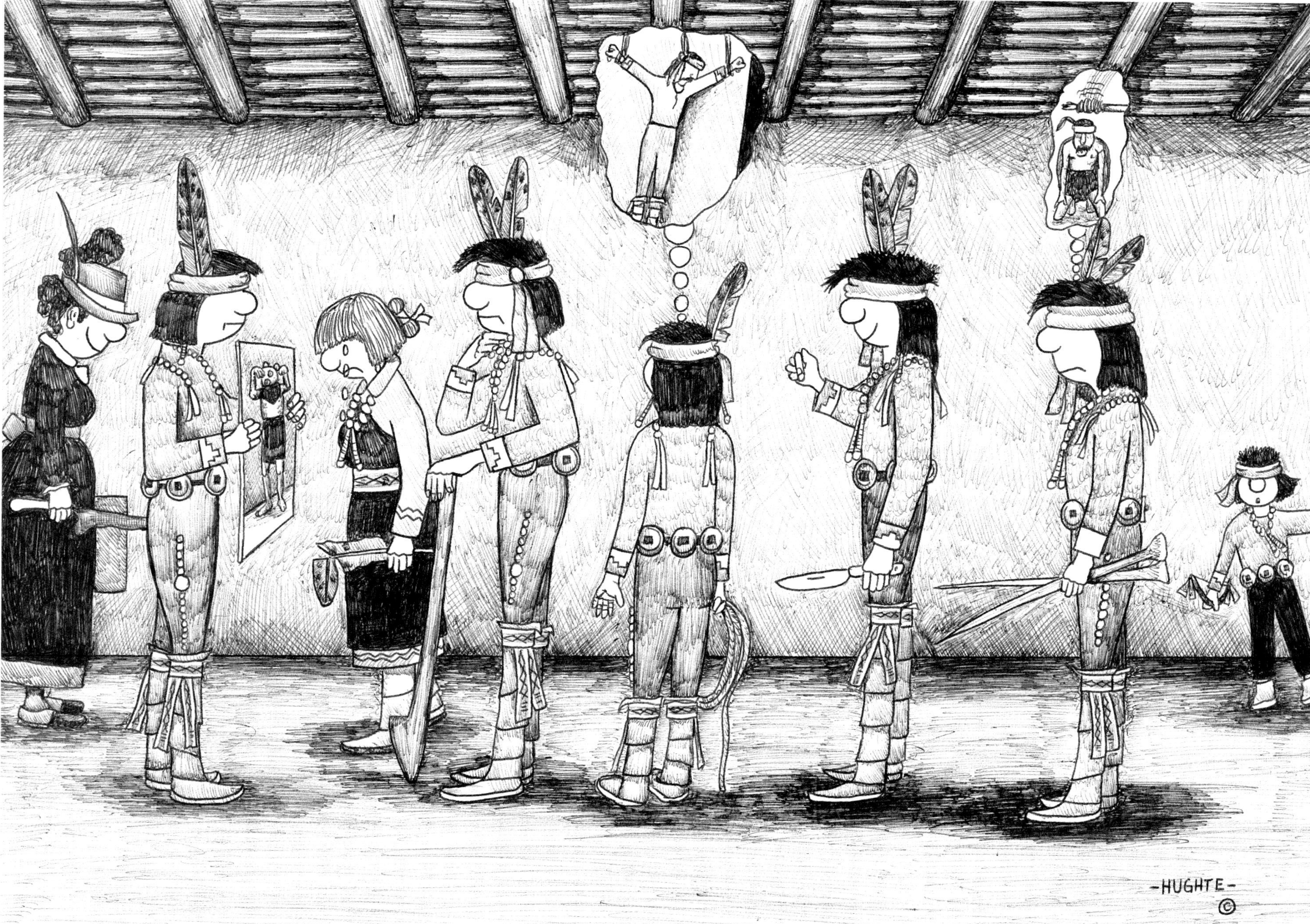
-HUGHTE-
©

Pálowahtiwa án-i
Hom pápa Pálowahtiwa, tem ta hom íyanikina témthla: Kóna ton téwanan áteaié? Élle tap ton i'-keetsana.

Téwanawe haw wéti; temta téwanawe haw lithl ton awen úlochnan tékwi yúasho a'shsha. Ténat k'yaki kowi ánaphoni'yunak'yanwaná! . . .
Ton áwen Sue,
Tenatsali

[My brother Palowahtiwa, also all my relatives, how are you these many days? If things are going well, you are all happy.

Every day I am sick, also here I am always lonesome for your country. Perhaps soon we shall see each other. . . .
Your younger brother,
Tenatsali]

—FHC letter to Palowahtiwa, after his final departure from Zuni, undated.

## The Last Supper——

*Cushing was sent to the Florida Keys to do his writings. He died in 1900 by eating a fish and swallowing a fish bone. On the bottom there is a black cat screaming at him. Notice that the feather is falling off. That is the end of Cushing. This was a fun drawing to do.*

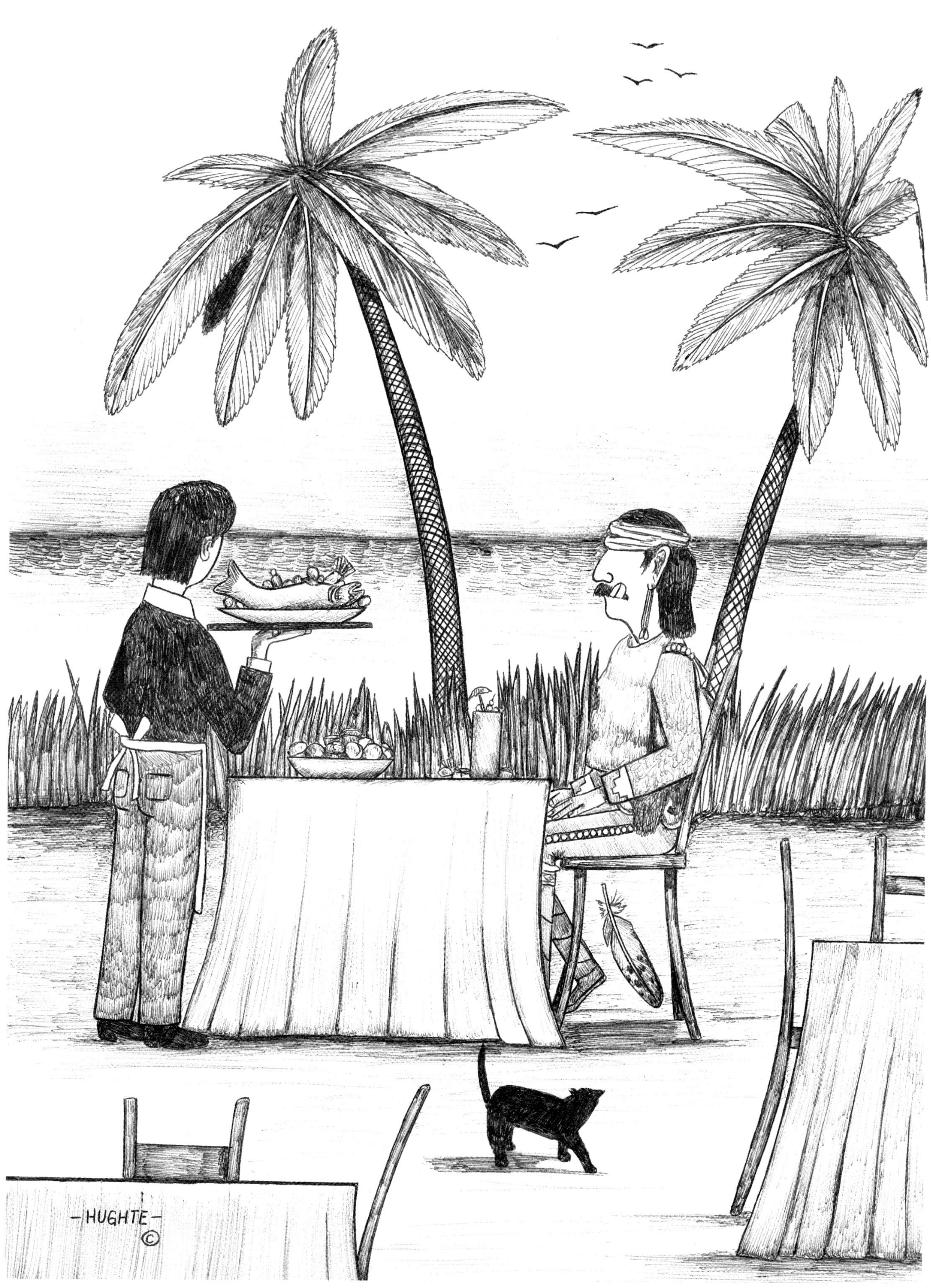
-HUGHTE-
©

# Reminiscing Cushing

*An elderly Zuni is reminiscing about Cushing and some of the funny things he did. He is talking about the time Cushing dressed as a Plains Indian and had his photo taken.*

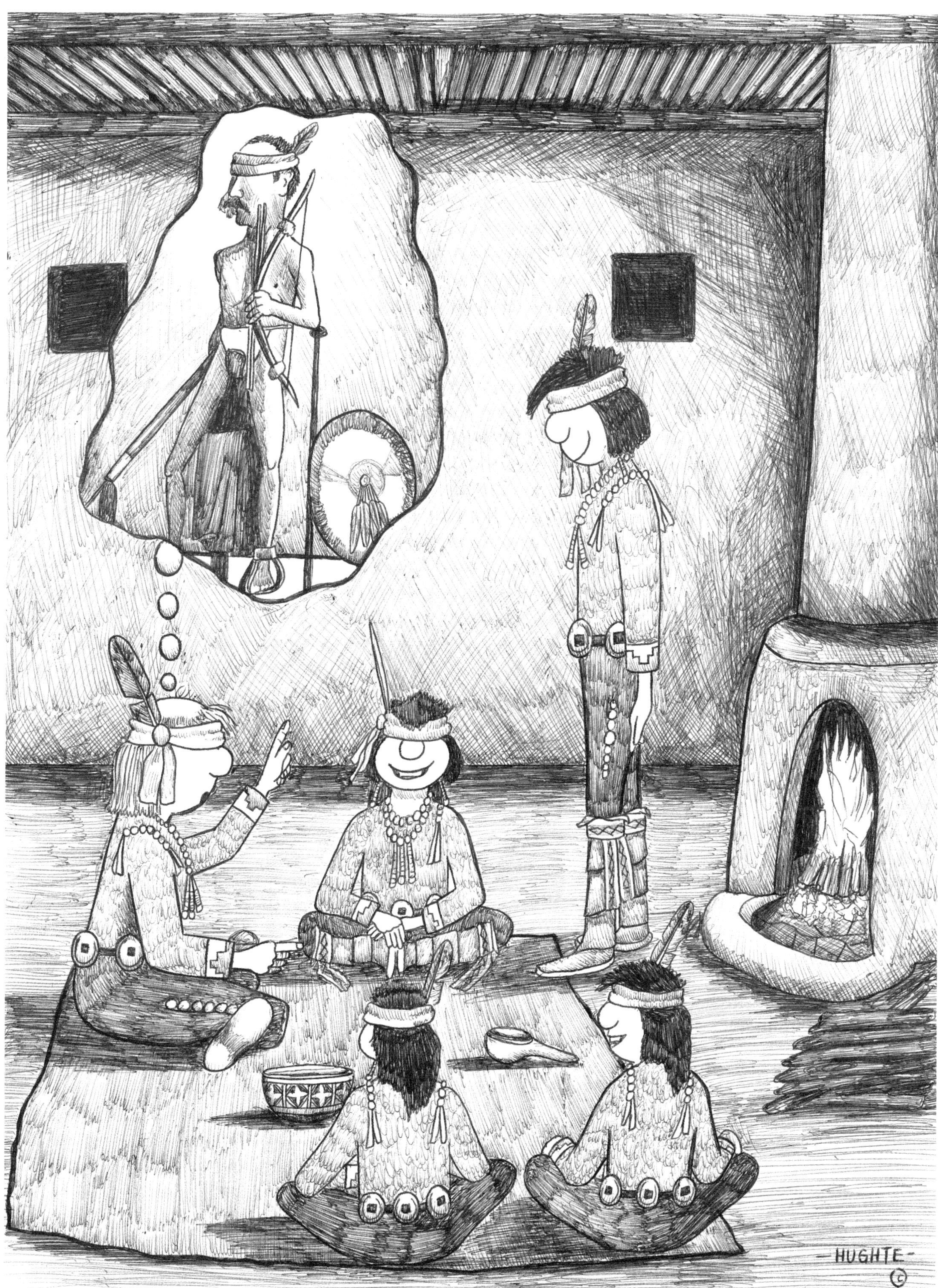
-HUGHTE-
©

# Chronology

*1857*
Frank Hamilton Cushing is born in Erie County, Pennsylvania, the sickly fourth son of a doctor. Three years later the family moves to New York State.

*1867*
At around the age of ten, Cushing becomes interested in Native Americans when he discovers his first artifact in the fields around his home. He makes himself an "Indian" costume and implements. Cushing later apparently recounted to William H. Holmes that he had also attempted to fly from a barn roof with the aid of wooden wings as a youngster.

*1874*
Briefly becomes a student at Cornell University.

*1875*
Appointed assistant curator at the Smithsonian Institution after having impressed Spencer Baird with a report on his archaeological findings which was published by the Smithsonian.

*1879*
Named as a member of the Smithsonian Bureau of Ethnology's first expedition to the Southwest, headed by Colonel James Stevenson. Also in the group is Stevenson's wife, Matilda, then an unpaid assistant but, after her husband's death, a Smithsonian ethnologist in her own right. The group is completed by photographer John Hillers.

***September 19th.*** Arrives in Zuni, the expeditions, first stop.

***September 27th.*** By this date Cushing is already a resident in the home of the governor Palowahtiwa, separating himself from the rest of the party that left for the Hopi pueblos within two weeks—leaving him with so few supplies that he comes to rely quickly on the generosity of his Zuni hosts.

***October.*** Soon after his arrival, Cushing meets We'wha, a friend of the two American teachers in Zuni. We'wha was a *lhamana*, a Zuni male who adopts female dress and roles. He was an important figure in Zuni life at the time while in later years also making an impact on Washington society as the guest of Matilda Coxe Stevenson.

***October 20th.*** The first of several incidents when Cushing's sketching and writing during a religious ceremony causes dancers and others to forcefully—yet unsuccessfully—attempt to stop him.

***December.*** Cushing is encouraged to adopt traditional Zuni clothing and has his ears pierced, the first stage of initiation. Later that month, he almost dies of exposure while exploring Zuni ruins and mines in the Zuni Mountains.

***1880***
***Spring.*** Learns conversational Zuni despite a bout of pneumonia and begins to publicly advocate the legitimacy of Zuni tribal rights.

***October 2nd.*** Cushing shoots at a herd of Navajo horses, the first of several similar episodes.

***1881***
***July.*** Returning from a visit to Havasupai in the Grand Canyon, Cushing obtains—in circumstances which were never fully explained—his first scalp, enabling him to be initiated into the Bow Priesthood.

*Fall.* Assumes the title of "1st War Chief."

*1882*
*Spring.* Cushing brings five Zunis and one Hopi to the East Coast where they visit Washington and Boston. Events during this trip included collecting water from the "Ocean of Sunrise," the attendance at many social functions including a meeting with President Chester Arthur, and Cushing's marriage to Emily Magill.

*November 1882–January 1883.* Cushing joins others in an expedition to the Hopi pueblos, primarily to acquire collections of artifacts.

*Fall 1882.* Two army officers and a civilian each stake a claim for 800 acres around Nutria, inadvertently omitted from maps of the Zuni Reservation. Cushing begins a campaign to have this land returned to the Zunis, a campaign which succeeded the following year despite the fact the the father-in-law of one of the soldiers concerned was the ranking Senator from Illinois, General John A. Logan.

*1883*
Cushing becomes more entrenched in Zuni, building a home and assisting in the defense of the community against a band of rustlers. He also continues his archaeological researches on behalf of the Smithsonian while beginning to "moonlight" as a private collector for the Berlin Museum and others. As he increasingly associates himself with the Zunis, the mutual rivalry and dislike between himself and Matilda Coxe Stevenson, the most prolific photographer of Zuni, increases. All the while, Cushing's health continues to be poor. The Nurtia Controversy continues.

*1884*
As a result of Cushing's protests against the actions of soldiers at Nutria, Senator Logan pressures the Smithsonian to have Cushing withdrawn from Zuni. This he finally accedes to in April 1884.

*1884–1886*
Cushing returns to the life of a curator at the Smithsonian. He replicates Zuni ceramics and ceremonial costumes, including a Mudhead mask which he is photographed wearing.

*1886–1889*
Director of the Hemenway Southwestern Archaeological Expedition, a privately-funded project aimed at excavating ancestral Zuni sites documenting the prehistoric migrations of the Zuni people. Ill health dogs Cushing, as does criticism of his leadership.

*1895–1896*
Financial support from his doctor who thought he needed a change of climate and, later, from Phoebe Hearst, allows Cushing to excavate at Key Marco in the Florida Keys. He finds many remarkable artifacts of wood, preserved in waterlogged deposits.

*1900*
Cushing chokes on a fish bone and dies. At the time he had been preparing the publication of archaeological investigations he conducted in Florida.

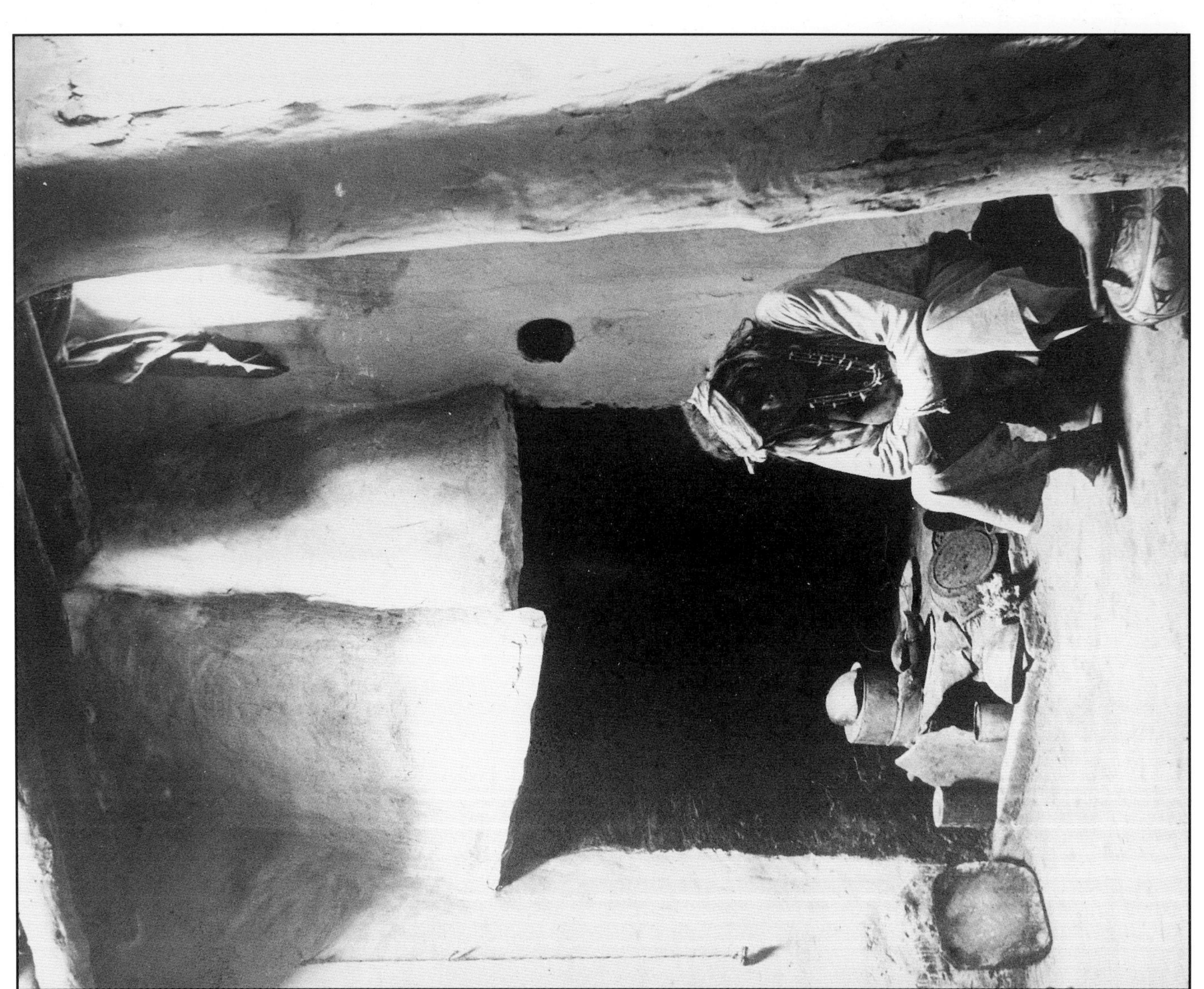

# Discourse

What follows was written by an outsider who has lived in Zuni for ten years. In 1984 I was hired by the governor and the council to establish an enterprise of the tribe to market Zuni arts and crafts. Over the course of the past ten years I have answered to three different councils for whatever the enterprise has done and for whatever the gossip network has said about it. My role has been less that of a trader and more that of an entrepreneur who works for the tribe and is charged with making as much money as possible in a way that is acceptable to the tribal council and to all of its 7,000-plus constituents. I have a staff of nine Zunis who alternately assist and direct me in this effort.

Early on I decided that if I were to reach the greatest number of Zunis, and therefore to most contribute to the industry of Zuni arts and crafts, I would have to remain unaligned and not be seen as an "adopted" member of any particular family. In Zuni terms if I were seen as working for the interests of one family then I would also be seen as neutral to—or even working against—the interests of another family. Zuni is a place where people unfriendly to each other can be brought together to prepare for a religious ceremony and afterwards say, "What a nice time we had working with people who we do not like." And it is a place where buying bread or gas can be a political statement. What this has meant is that I have adopted a less personal style than Frank Cushing; rather than having "brothers" or "sisters," "fathers" or "mothers" at Zuni I have only friends—and moderate enemies. The strength of this position is that I can function well as a mediator between craftspeople, between members of our staff, and between the council and the tribal enterprise. The weakness of the position is that I am never sure who will agree with me, and (if they agree) whether they will give their support.

This book of Cushing cartoons started with a discussion of Zuni humor between Phil Hughte and myself which had been prompted by a previous discussion with Krisztina Kosse about Native American humor. Phil had drawn some cartoons placing Zunis in the context of Stonehenge, the Statue of Liberty, and the Golden Gate. These cartoons had placed Zunis in foreign cultural settings, specifically in the world of Whitemen. As Phil and I talked about these drawings, we also talked about Whitemen in the world of Zunis and this led us directly to a discussion of THE Whiteman in Zuni, Frank Hamilton Cushing.

Both of us then knew that Cushing had to be the subject of future cartoons. As Phil would complete two or three cartoons he would excitedly bring them to the store to show me, to explain their meaning, and to sell them. Then we would brainstorm other possible subjects for Cushing cartoons. Sometimes those brainstorms resulted in cartoons and sometimes not. It was clear that Phil was looking for ideas as to how he might represent

Cushing and that what he selected as subject matter had to be humorous and had to fit what he imagined in the meeting between Cushing and Zuni. What began as a few cartoons on Cushing turned into a collection of forty-three drawings chronicling Cushing's life. Not wishing to sell them piecemeal, yet not knowing what else to do with them, the cartoons sat in a box under my desk for the next six months. A little later I showed them to Krisztina and she thought them both funny and substantial and the idea of an exhibit and monograph arose. The Maxwell Museum and the new Zuni museum—A:shiwi A:wan Museum and Heritage Center—were enlisted to help mount the exhibit.

What I have tried to understand from the cartoons and from the letters of Cushing that Jesse Green has admirably compiled in the book *Cushing at Zuni: The Correspondence and Journals of Frank Hamilton Cushing, 1879–1884* (see Readings) is why the Zunis responded in the way they did to this singular Whiteman at this period in their history.

The meeting between Zunis and Cushing was a meeting between old and young, between Zuni and white American, between accomplished and neophyte, between a village of insiders and a single outsider, between the collected and the collector, between Zuni and the United States, and between those with an enormous past trying to glimpse the present and those with little past only looking to the future. The Zuni that I have met is not the same Zuni that Cushing met. There are many Whitemen who are now living in or have lived in Zuni since Cushing. Almost all Zunis—craftspeople, council, tribal administrators—are skilled in dealing with them. It is not the same Zuni, and yet as I read Cushing's correspondence and see this very young man puzzled by his experiences in the village I can easily envision his position.

Zuni is a small and isolated village of 8,000 which behaves as if it were an independent country of 100,000. It lies thirty-three miles south of an interstate highway and occupies the same land that it had when Cushing first visited and probably occupied a thousand years before that. Zuni continues to operate as a separate country (not a village) with its own language, its own government, and its own traditions. How is it that such a small number of people can maintain this separate identity and cultural independence, especially in the face of aggressive, expansionist, and often haughty representatives of Anglo-American culture? Clearly there is a Zuni way of doing things, there are Zuni responses to issues of aesthetics or art or politics or land, and clearly the Zunis have developed a social system which reinforces, maintains, and adapts these values. It is not the same Zuni that Cushing knew, but the remarkable thing is that what I understand to have been the Zuni responses to Cushing have much in common with the responses I have experienced. It may not be the same Zuni but whatever it is that created those responses is the same Zuni.

Cushing came to Zuni in 1879 as a young man of twenty-two. He was assistant curator for the Smithsonian Institution. His assigned task was to collect artifacts from a village representative of traditional Pueblo culture. Before coming to Zuni, Cushing had been an exhibit preparator and had been involved in some archaeological excavation. He had no previous ethnographic experience, nor had he been to the Southwest.

Cushing was expected to collect singular examples of Zuni material culture (pottery, textiles, carvings, and religious objects), to describe those objects in the field, and to gain an understanding of Zuni culture and society. The intellectual premise for this enterprise which shaped the "how" and the "why" of Cushing's expedition was twofold: it was believed that American Indian societies would soon be overcome by the larger, more aggressive American society; and that cultures are evolutionary in character and that the culture of the Pueblos represented an earlier, less evolved stage than Anglo-American culture. These two premises were used to justify two further beliefs: if a less advanced culture were about to be overcome by a more advanced one, then the collecting agency should salvage as much as possible without particular concern about the consequences of such an activity on indigenous societies; and a more advanced society had the intellectual right—in the name of Science—to investigate a less advanced society, in order to study its evolutionary past.

> *Major Powell left for the Grand Cañon yesterday, but before he went we talked the Oraibi matter over fully, and he has instructed me to secure your cooperation and the Mindeleff's party and "clean out" Oraibi—ethnologically speaking. Now my dear fellow, we don't want any "flair" about this. You and I will quietly go over to Keam's Cañon and from there to Oraibi and see what we can do in the way of making a tidy little collection. But remember, the less we have to say about it, the fewer annoying questions we will have to answer and the less criticism we will provoke from "certain" sources* (letter to Cushing from Joseph Stanley-Brown, 1882, in Green 1990:247–8)

J. Stanley-Brown was secretary to Major Powell, the director of the Bureau of Ethnology, and would later serve as private secretary to President Garfield. Clearly, such views carried with them the intellectual baggage of paternalism, elitism, and even racism.

In September 1879 a young man of modest education, no previous experience either in the West or with any Native American group, of frail health and somewhat impetuous in nature was left behind at Zuni Pueblo to fend for himself. He was charged with collecting art and artifacts for the Smithsonian. He didn't know the language and had no more than a passing familiarity with the culture. In this part of the West, the 1880s were a time of American expansion, a time of increased stress on Zuni society, and subsequently of increasing suspicion of outsiders. Cushing had virtually no charter to conduct this collecting activity other than a piece of paper which said that he was collecting for the Smithsonian Institution, the National Museum of the United States. Clearly, in such a setting, whatever was to be accomplished for the Smithsonian had to be improvised by the collector . . . and this is what Cushing did during his four-year residence among the Zuni people.

What came to pass in this setting is that Cushing came to serve three masters: the Smithsonian Institution, his Zuni benefactors, and his own personal and intellectual ambitions as a new breed of American ethnologist. That these three masters were in intellectual and practical conflict I think his letters leave no doubt. I also think that his attempt to satisfy all three masters caused much of his difficulty at the Pueblo and would cause at least two of the masters to turn against him. He was recalled by the Smithsonian and plots formed against him at Zuni. What became at issue was loyalty: the more he tried to be loyal to each of his masters, the less he was believed to be loyal by any of them and the more he was given to feelings of being used and eventually betrayed by each of them.

Conflicting loyalties, I think, also lie at the heart of the intellectual premise of modern ethnology—namely, "participant observation," which argues that a researcher should have the intimacy of a participant and the objectivity of an observer in order to understand a culture. What is missed, in my opinion, in this search for objective ethnology is that adherence to the intellectual premise of participant observation compromises the group that is being researched. In my view participant observation is an armchair conceit: it tries to place a framework for getting "inside" information, but fails to recognize how the act of recording, and then divulging what is recorded, can undermine the society being investigated. It is a matter (certainly it was for the Zunis) of divulging "secrets" of participants in religious societies by one who was a participant; it is also the telling of "secrets" to an outsider by anyone who is Zuni. Such acts are by their nature disloyal—a Zuni religious participant telling of his religious society, a lover telling of his or her paramour, a politician telling about fellow congressmen, or an anthropologist simply reporting what was seen as an insider. In other words, the disloyalty stems from rendering public what was a private activity in which one willingly engaged. More than discretion is expected; it has to do with loyalty to the group such that one's subsequent activities (or revelations) do not serve to undermine the group.

If there were ever a society defined by its loyalties I suspect it is Zuni. And if there were ever a society which is less defined by its loyalties I suspect it has to be modern America. In Zuni there are loyalties to immediate family, to extended family, to clan, to kiva group, to medicine society, and to religious society. There is no statute of limitation on these loyalties. In the case of family and clan they begin at birth, in the case of kiva or religious society they begin at initiation, and they never cease. There is no exit from these responsibilities and no severance from the loyalty expected. In contrast, American society expects loyalty to immediate family (but not extended family), loyalty to one's employer as long as one is employed, loyalty to one's wife as long as one is married, loyalty to one's friends as long as they are friendly, and loyalty to one's group as long as one is a member of that group. Loyalties of modern American can be characterized as conditional and are in effect only as long as one is a member. The exception to this conditional loyalty is the loyalty extended to immediate family (particularly to parents and children) and to country. In America discontinued loyalty to either immediate family or to country is seen as disloyalty and may even be labeled traitorous. In all other modern American associations, the discontinuance of membership is expected and loyalties only extend to the time that one is an actual member. (Thus when promotion for the vice-president of Ford does not come in a timely manner he can switch to the presidency of Chrysler without undue criticism.) For a member of an extended family, clan, or an initiated society in Zuni there is no cessation of loyalties. They are not conditional on health, money, or time. When duty calls, a Zuni is expected to answer.

Cushing cultivated loyalties at Zuni in order to gain access to goods and information for the Smithsonian and it is clear that Zunis were being used by the Smithsonian (and Cushing) to further its own interests as a repository of goods and information about Pueblo cultures. Cushing also cultivated Zunis to cement his position as interpreter and expositor on Zuni culture. Thus, his friendship with the governor was not cultivated because of his desire to strengthen civil government, nor was his recording of ritual done to strengthen the societies using that ritual, nor did his cultivation of (and eventual initiation into) the Bow Priests stem from his wish to strengthen that institution but rather from his desire to gain access to more information about Zuni social structure and her secret institutions.

Did he act as a spy? No, not in the sense that he sought to gain information that might be used against the Zunis. Did he act as a cultural spy? Perhaps, insofar as he believed in the evolutionary theories of Lewis Henry Morgan and sought to use the information from Zuni as evidence of the more "primitive" stage of Zuni and the "more evolved" position of his own society. This was information which when placed in a framework could be used to strengthen the social institutions of Anglo-American society and, if believed (by Zunis or outsiders—school teachers, Bureau of Indian Affairs bureaucrats, missionaries, government officials, soldiers, or American entrepreneurs), to undermine the social institutions of Zuni.

Still further, perhaps he was a cultural spy in the sense that he sought to take that which was secretly held by the Zunis to outsiders and that which was secretly held by one religious society of Zuni and render it public. This sense of spying has less to do with undermining that which is spied upon as indifference to the undermining . . . as in the case of the *paparazzi* sneaking photos of the British Royal Family or of a reporter publishing the private life of his political subject.

I see no evidence that these were questions Cushing debated with himself or with others. Clearly, in matters of acquiring information and artifacts, Cushing's loyalties were pre-eminently to the Smithsonian Institution and to the "science" of ethnology. But, as with any maturing person, Cushing appears to have experienced a shifting of loyalties—a strengthening of his loyalty to the Zuni people (and their institutions), a strengthening of his loyalty to his personal ambition, and a weakening of his loyalty to the institutions of the Smithsonian and the Bureau of Ethnology.

As evidence of his growing loyalty to the social institutions of the Zunis I would cite the newspaper interview Cushing gave to the *Washington Evening News* in 1892 (Green 1990: 340–2) wherein he describes the occurrences of witches in Zuni, the extraction of confessions, and the punishments. Even though a newspaper had reported that two Zuni women had been executed for practicing sorcery he made the case that "there is no truth to the report," that the U.S. Government made a grave error in sending troops to Zuni, and that the troops should be recalled immediately. He went on to state that "sorcery in Zuni does not wholly depend upon superstitious beliefs" and that he had known several sorcerers who were better characterized as "anarchists of primitive life." He continued, "it is their endeavor to overcome the sacred assemblies [and in so doing] they resort . . . to violence and very frequently to actual poisoning."

Despite his mixed loyalties, in the end it was the Smithsonian Institution and not the Zunis that asked Cushing to leave. If the Zunis had so desired, they could easily have expelled him. No subterfuge would have been required (at most only a modest pretext) as Zunis have consistently shown with other outsiders—Bureau of Indian Affairs officials, anthropologists, traders, and missionaries. Regardless of the power, real or illusory, of an outsider (Cushing included), single outsiders represent no threat to the life of the Pueblo. They are not Zunis.

What did the Zunis want? Why did they take this awkward foreigner to live with them? Why did they allow him to remain? Why did they allow him to take notes (and even make drawings) of their dances? Why did they give him information about their sacred sites and the meanings of their religious traditions? Why did they try to marry him to a Zuni woman? Why did they initiate him into one of their secret societies? In short, why did they give him access to the Pueblo of Zuni?

First, it should be noted that the Zunis did not invite Cushing to the Pueblo. They did not ask the Smithsonian Institution to place an ethnologist among them to study and record their practices. Cushing simply arrived, a Whiteman who did not speak their language and who apparently had ties with a government which had been sporadically active in this area of the Southwest since its successful campaign against the Navajos. Cushing was no Esteban who happened onto Zuni and immediately made demands, nor was he a priestly representative of a foreign power who wished to educate and convert, nor was he head of a military expedition from the most recent colonizing power. He came by himself, by mule. He was thin, young, had little money, no charter from a stronger power, no real ability to defend himself. He asked for nothing but to live in the Pueblo and to be a friend. He represented no threat. There was nothing about him that suggested anything to fear. Since there was nothing imposing about him there was no reason to fear being imposed upon. Why shouldn't the Zunis invite him to share some of their food and their shelter? If problems arose he could be turned away easily enough. It should also be noted that there was no vote among the Zunis to allow Cushing to stay. There was no polling of religious societies to see if Cushing's objectives were compatible with their own. In the beginning there was not even an opportunity for the gossip network to render its evaluation of the man and his purposes. It appears that the decision to allow Cushing to stay was largely a personal one: the governor of Zuni, Palowahtiwa, took a personal liking to him and offered him shelter.

Initially, I think the decision was no more than one individual taking a liking to another, offering a place to stay, and looking forward to conversation and pleasant social interaction. But, of course, this was the governor of the Pueblo, a man charged with its civil administration. Palowahtiwa was familiar with Americans, and may well have thought that Cushing might be one American whom the Zunis could use, and the governor himself might use in some as yet undetermined way to work for the interests of his own political faction. And, besides, the governor may have thought that if things didn't work out,this young American could always be asked to leave.

One of the singular things about Zunis, especially in contrast to other Pueblo people or Navajos, is their lack of fear of strangers. My own sense of it is that it has to do with the confidence they have in their social institutions and their traditions, and in the pride they have for things that are Zuni. I think that it also has to do with the fact that they live in a place where they have lived for a thousand years. They have been on a primary north-south trade route since prehistoric times and this trade has accustomed them to dealing with strangers. It is easy for Zunis to act on equal, if not superior footing to all whom they meet. It is easy for Zunis to extend friendship and—something that I think Cushing never learned—it is easy for them to withdraw friendship. Given this, what had the governor to lose by extending his friendship to young Cushing in the fall of 1879?

Unlike the lifetime obligations to family, clan, and religious societies, friendship at Zuni is something that can easily be extended to outsiders. There is an ease to Zuni friendship in that responsibilities are minimal; it exists as long as two people desire it and it can be broken when one person desires it end. (Marriages at Zuni might be seen as a form of friendship: when the friendship of husband and wife ends the children stay with the mother in her home and the husband goes home to his mother.) It is particularly easy for Zunis to extend friendship to outsiders where there are almost no commitments. Should the friendship sour it is the outsider, not the Zuni, who goes home to his "mother." Zunis may take an immediate liking to an outsider and act in a most pleasant manner, as if their history together were of considerable depth, and then break it off with an almost guiltless dispatch. It is not that Zuni friendships are of short duration, nor that there is something scheming to them, but they are almost like a business relationship in Anglo-American society where each party feigns a real depth to the relationship while knowing that if "business" turns down or a better offer is made by a competing firm the relationship may end with barely a murmur.

If the other social institutions of Zuni have no exit, friendship at Zuni is filled with so many exits that departure is effected simply by leaving. And just as in business, friendships at Zuni can easily be restarted when interests are mutual.

In the fall of 1879, when Cushing was looking for Zunis to bond with and to assist him in his work, as he had with Spencer Baird at the Smithsonian and would with Washington Matthews and John Bourke—Zunis may not at all have been looking to bond with a lonely Anglo who arrived at the Pueblo. Perhaps, they were only extending the pleasantries of Zuni friendship without incurring any of its obligations as in Anglo-American society. It should be noted that in all those relationships where Cushing felt the warmth of friendship while in Zuni—Baird, Bourke, Matthews, Dubois, Baxter, and Palowahtiwa—his relationships were open, easy, and productive to both sides. But, in all those relationships where friendship was missing—Stevenson, Logan, (to some degree Powell), and Luna—his relationships were characterized by doubt, suspicion, fear, antagonism and sometimes hatred. As the relationship between the Zunis and Cushing became warmer their relationship shifted from that of friends to quasi-relatives. One finds Cushing and certain Zunis using the locutions of "little brother," "son," and "father." From the Zuni point of view this acknowledges that something more than friendship is wanted, something more is expected; at the same time this fictionalized relationship could be stopped with Cushing "sent home to his mother." Palowahtiwa addresses Cushing as follows:

> *Unless you are a fool, you shall be poor no longer. You shall have brothers, sisters; I and mine; uncles and aunts; fathers and mothers; and where such are, no man need be poor* (reminiscence by Cushing, 1890, in Green 1990: 41).

I can remember my own coming to Zuni. I had been hired to organize and run a new tribal business to market Zuni arts. I had told a Zuni friend that I was going to Zuni alone, that I would live by myself in a house in the village, and that I would be in the employ of the tribal council. Her immediate reaction was to say, "Oh, poor Jim, there will be no one for you."

The relationships between Anglo-Americans and Native Americans have always been characterized by the Anglo-Americans searching for the "person" who made decisions. If a Native American community would not or could not identify a single individual who was "in charge" then the Americans would appoint someone with that title, that is, they would appoint a "boss." What is remarkable about a community like Zuni is not the lack of bosses but rather the preponderance of them. What is remarkable in a Pueblo society described as a theocratic autocracy (W. W. *Hill: Ethnography of Santa Clara Pueblo New Mexico,* edited and annotated by Charles H. Lange, p.190), and thus supposedly undemocratic in form, is the large number of people who make decisions that affect the rest: governors, ex-governors, councilmen, ex-councilmen, kiva leaders, medicine society leaders, fraternity leaders, advocacy groups, administrators, ex-administrators, silversmiths, and educators. In a supposedly "closed" society like Zuni there may well be more opportunities for leadership than there are in an "open" society like modern America. The corollary to this plethora of leaders is the number of people who are investing in the system, each playing a separate role in the maintenance of the system. The genius of Zuni is that by having so many important investors—so many bosses—the threat of anarchy is virtually eliminated. Another corollary is that the greatest threat to the Zuni system is the indigenous anarchists—namely, the witches. Strong efforts are made to remove the anarchists. In fact, an important role of witches is to contrast the disorder of non-Zuni life with the order of life that is Zuni.

Not long after I started working at Zuni an award ceremony was taking place in front of the tribal building and one of the Anglo anthropologists in the ceremony came running into the store excitedly asking for a camera. He said, "Your boss wants you to take a picture." Without thinking I asked "Which one?" He meant the governor, but I meant which one of the hundreds of Zunis was he referring to who in their daily lives act as "The Boss" of the tribal arts and crafts business.

We should not assume that Cushing's acceptance by the governor of Zuni or his initiation as a Bow Priest meant he was accepted by the majority of Zunis. Both were significant events, but, with the exception of Luna, we don't know what the other "bosses" said or thought about this importunate and awkward American. Most importantly we don't have access to Zuni gossip about Cushing. For Cushing's stay at Zuni we have access to his letters, to the letters from his superiors in Washington, and to his writings. We don't know what the Zunis really thought of him as a slight and often sickly "Melican" with some kind of connection to Washington D.C. What did they think of his making notes and drawings of religious events, of the clothing he wore or his activities in the defense of Zuni? What was thought about his ties with certain Zuni families and not others, of his childlike behavior, and especially of his initiation into the Bow Priesthood? None of this is part of the record. It is in the gossip, more than in any other place, where Frank Cushing's relationship to the people of Zuni would be most revealed. At Zuni it matters not so much whether or not gossip is true. What matters is what is said, what questions are asked, what doubts are raised, what assertions expressed. At Zuni all individuals in the Pueblo are tried by the public opinion of Zuni gossip. Despite the autocracy of a place like Zuni (or rather because of it) gossip is at its most egalitarian; no person—no governor, no religious leader, no politician, no outsider—is immune.

I don't know any gossip about Cushing which still circulates. In my ten years at Zuni I have heard none. The only references I have heard about Cushing have been directed at former Zuni leaders who allowed this "Melican" to be initiated as a Bow Priest, not at Cushing himself. A political leader under intellectual siege by another faction for not following Zuni ways countered that at least neither he nor his allies were responsible for initiating an outsider as his predecessors had done. Why did the Zunis initiate Cushing as a Bow Priest? This initiation still bothers Zunis and no outsider since Cushing has been initiated. Although Cushing was initiated we can infer that it was not acceptable to all Zunis. My guess is that his initiation was a pragmatic decision made by a few Zunis who believed that they could use this "Melican" for their own ends, perhaps to buffer Zuni from the onslaught of other outsiders. Unlike other outsiders—military leaders, missionaries, ranchers—Cushing didn't come to change Zuni or to take its land. Certainly he displayed his loyalty to the people of Zuni through his attentiveness, his dress, his sharing of the pleasures and the rigors of Zuni life. He acted differently from other Anglo visitors and, though his actions were often uncouth, he tried, nonetheless, to adapt the proper form and he appears to have genuinely cared for the Zunis he befriended. In a photograph of Cushing seated with the Zunis he took East, I note the casual manner in which his arm rests on the knee of Palowahtiwa who in fact had taught him the ritual of the Bow Priesthood. It seems a most natural gesture, denoting ease and bonds of friendship. It also speaks of the conduit by which an outsider is brought into a Zuni secret society charged with protecting Zuni people from the threat of outsiders.

When I asked an elderly Zuni whom I have known for years what he thought of Cushing, he said:

> *He was a good man. I was told that although he was a Whiteman he behaved like a Zuni. I was told that he lived with other pious men [Zuni religious leaders] and when that happens one begins to believe in things like Zuni religion. I was told that that happened to him. I heard that when there was raiding by Navajos in the West, they would steal livestock and sometimes kill the sheep herders. I heard that Cushing went with a group of Zunis and he killed one of the raiders. I think it*

> *was that reason that he became a Bow Priest . . . for when you do something like that or kill a bear, then the clan takes immediate steps—does not wait a day—to initiate.*

On the other hand, for many Zunis, Cushing's initiation was an anomalous act and one can still find older Zunis who when under attack by their kinsmen will say, "Well, whatever it is alleged that we have done, at least we did not initiate an outsider."

One of the early ideas for this book was to include Zuni views of Cushing and to that end we solicited responses from older Zunis, young adults, and school children. When the cartoons were displayed in Zuni we had placed a book at the exit asking for responses from visitors. We were hoping to overhear Zuni gossip but what has become clear was that though Cushing has entered village history and though no anthropologist or even Anglo has greater name recognition we did not overhear any gossip about this man, Frank Cushing. In a sense, Phil Hughte, through his making of the Cushing cartoons, has become the Zuni scholar of Frank Cushing. Phil's comments are as close as what we can have on Zuni gossip about Cushing. In overhearing Zuni comments on the cartoons what also became clear is that Cushing's place in Zuni history is not fixed, and is still being reviewed by Zunis as an instance of both an anthropologist and an Anglo who participated significantly in Zuni life.

Jim Ostler
February 4, 1994
Zuni

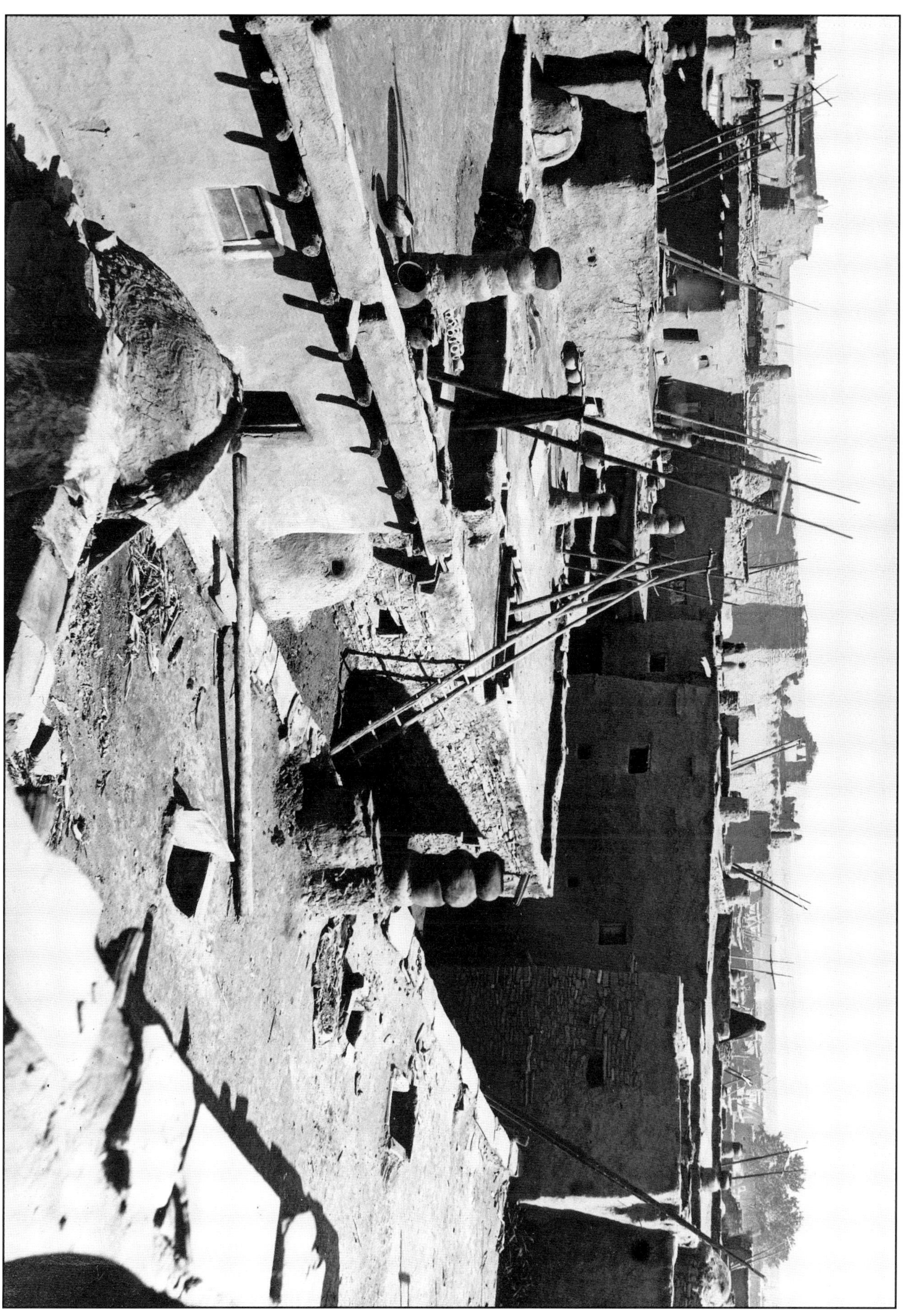

# Commentary

Looking at Phil Hughte's cartoons is like peeling back a pleasing, beautifully formed but pungent onion. There is the aesthetic pleasure of form and texture, there is the intellectual pleasure of peeling back layers of meaning, there are the emotional ups and downs of tears and laughter, and there is, as in all good cartoons, a bite.

The aesthetic pleasure comes from a combination of unfussy, precisely controlled lines and a richness of detail. The clarity of line combined with a wealth of detail provides movement and interest but does not overwhelm. These opposites also reinforce the emotional ambiguity of the drawings. For what the artist wanted to say no existing genre served well enough, so Phil Hughte invented his own: the pictures are combinations of cartoons and drawings. There is a punch, but it is tempered with kindness and the sheer pleasure of showing the details of Zuni life. The drawings could stand by themselves, but as a series, the whole is greater than the parts. There is sweetness, but there is also judgment.

At their simplest, the cartoons/drawings are a narrative of Cushing's life. A young ethnologist, Cushing was sent to study a typical southwestern pueblo by the Smithsonian Institution in 1879 as a member of Colonel James Stevenson's collecting expedition. Cushing soon separated from the rest of the party and moved in with the governor of Zuni. Originally told to stay three months, Cushing stayed for more than four years. During his stay he learnt the language, adopted Zuni dress, and eventually became a member of the Bow Priest Society. Phil Hughte tells the story of Cushing, self-proclaimed "1st War Chief of Zuni, and U.S. Assistant Ethnologist." In Cushing's writings all Zunis speak through Cushing. In the cartoons, Hughte takes Cushing's writings as a starting point and reinterprets them through his knowledge of Zuni.

The drawings are above all about Zuni: how Zunis live and how they see the world. Hughte's Zuni appears as a place in seemingly constant motion. There is some action and also some further action implied in almost every drawing. The most important actions are those that have consequences for other people. As most acts touch somebody else, life becomes a process of daily negotiations and renegotiations between people. Hence the feeling of ceaseless motion. Life also seems to unfold through the many actions of everyday comings and goings. There is rhythm, vitality, and also humor as each act is evaluated and judged.

To an outsider, Zuni seems remote and isolated from the world. Looking at Hughte's cartoons is like looking through the other end of a telescope. In the cartoons the center of the world is Zuni and the rest of the world the periphery. The

Zuni of the cartoons is self-sufficient, confident, but hardly isolated from the world. The outside is brought in, evaluated and filtered, and meshed into the whole: a different place, but an engaged and active part of the world. The view does indeed depend on the perspective. What seemed near is now far, and what seemed remote is now the heart of the world.

Beyond inverting our view and showing a different perspective, the cartoons also make evaluations and judgments on a more general level. It is true that much of the humor comes from the Zuni's reaction to Cushing's un-Zunilike behavior: his sleeping in a hammock instead on the floor, his appearance and excruciating thinness, his being constantly cold, his constant rushing about, etc. But beyond poking fun at cultural differences, Phil Hughte goes deeper and evaluates the man by yardsticks we can all recognize. It is to Hughte's credit that Cushing emerges in the drawings not as a caricature but as a human being. He has faults aplenty, yes, but also some virtues and human vulnerabilities.

In some ways, Cushing's extraordinary success as an ethnologist was the result of his extraordinary insensitivity as a man. He jumped in where today's more sensitive angels would very much fear to tread. Despite a certain lack of sensitivity, Hughte's Cushing did his jumping with such exuberance that we cannot help but share some of his joy in finding such an interesting and wonderful place as Zuni. Paradoxically, Hughte's Cushing emerges as childlike and as a man of supreme confidence. In many ways Cushing was like a child: he ran around ceaselessly, was always curious, poked his nose in places where he was not wanted, and enjoyed all the attention he could get at both Zuni and outside. What do you do with this bright but importunate childlike man? You could cut his head off, hang him, castrate him, or initiate him. The Zunis decided to initiate him, in the hope that he would "learn better."

Cushing also possessed enormous self-confidence. He was a man of his time and culture and believed in the rationality of the human mind and the value of the pursuit of knowledge. He was able to live in two worlds and pass between them without an identity crisis. It probably did not occur to him that he could have one. Cushing's experience would be difficult to repeat today. Today's world is more self-questioning and also more self-conscious. Anthropologists, especially, seem like the Hamlets of today: they understand that even with the best intentions in the world actions may have unwanted consequences; they also more often question their own motivations. While self-doubt and self-examination may be commendable, they are also inhibiting. Cushing's contribution to ethnology—gained through a mixture of extraordinary sensitivity toward the intricacies of Zuni life and thought and a near total in sensitivity toward what should and should not be revealed—remains unique and probably unrepeatable today.

Cushing could be an ethnologist and a Zuni without seemingly agonizing over whether or not he was doing the right thing. He knew he was. The Zunis sympathize and even like him, but they are also fully aware of his shortcomings. Phil Hughte makes fun of Cushing's pretensions, his vanity and his self-centeredness. There is the irony of Cushing and Emily teaching the Zunis how to enter a house in a place that has been home for centuries. There is Cushing who loves to dress up—the more exotic the better. There is also Cushing, with his diagrams on how to make prayer sticks, teaching the world what it is like to be a Zuni. But beyond the ironies and forgivable failings, Cushing also fails at crucial points.Revealing sacred knowledge for passing fame, Cushing comes close to betrayal. This one sin was unforgivable. Phil Hughte's laughter mixes with some tears.

The onion probably contains many more layers than have been peeled off here. But beyond the different layers that may be read differently by different people, is there a solid, non-opaque core to the cartoons? I suggest the core is our common humanity. We all admire virtue and abhor vice. In rare moments of clarity, we also recognize that we are all fallible. What we would hate above all else is a perfect human being. Phil Hughte's Cushing—curious, insensitive, bright, courageous, greedy, and vain—escapes such an undesirable fate.

Krisztina Kosse
Curator of Collections
University of New Mexico
Maxwell Museum of Anthropology

# Readings

Bender, Norman J., ed. 1984. *Missionaries, Outlaws and Indians: Taylor F. Ealy at Lincoln and Zuni, 1878–1881.* Albuquerque: University of New Mexico Press.

Crampton, C. Gregory. 1977. *The Zunis of Cibola.* Salt Lake City: University of Utah Press.

Cushing, Frank Hamilton. [1882–83] 1967. *My Adventures in Zuni.* Reprint. Palmer Lake, Colorado: Filter Press.

Cushing, Frank Hamilton. [1883] 1974. *Zuni Fetishes.* Reprint. Las Vegas: KC Publications.

Cushing, Frank Hamilton. [1884–5] 1974. *Zuni Breadstuff.* Reprint. New York: Museum of the American Indian, Heye Foundation.

Cushing, Frank Hamilton. [1901] 1992. *Zuni Folk Tales.* Reprint. Tucson: University of Arizona Press.

Eggan, Fred, and Triloki Nath Pandey. 1979. Zuni History, 1850–1970. In vol. 9 of *Handbook of North American Indians,* ed. William C. Sturtevant. Washington, D.C.: Smithsonian Institution Press.

Fane, Diana. 1983. New questions for "old things": The Brooklyn Museum's Zuni Collections. In *The Early Years of Native American Art History,* ed. Janet C. Berlo. Seattle: University of Washington Press.

Ferguson, T.J., and E. Richard Hart. 1985. *A Zuni Atlas.* Norman: University of Oklahoma Press.

Green, Jesse, ed. 1979. *Zuni: Selected Writings of Frank Hamilton Cushing.* Lincoln: University of Nebraska Press.

Green, Jesse, ed. 1990. *Cushing at Zuni: the Correspondence and Journals of Frank Hamilton Cushing, 1879–1884.* Albuquerque: University of New Mexico Press.

Hinsley, Curtis M., Jr. 1981. *Savages and Scientists: The Smithsonian Institution and the Development of American Anthropology, 1846–1910.* Washington, D.C.: Smithsonian Institution Press.

Hinsley, Curtis M., Jr. 1983. Ethnographic charisma and scientific routine: Cushing and Fewkes in the American Southwest, 1879–1893. In *Observers Observed: Essays on Ethnographic Fieldwork,* ed. George W. Stocking. Madison: University of Wisconsin Press.

Hovens, Pieter. 1988. The anthropologist as enigma: Frank Hamilton Cushing. *European Review of Native American Studies* 2(1): 1–5.

Mark, Joan. 1980. *Four Anthropologists: An American Science in its Early Years.* New York: Science History Publications.

Mindeleff, Victor. [1891] 1989. *A Study of Pueblo Architecture in Tusayan and Cibola.* Reprint. Washington, D.C.: Smithsonian Institution Press.

Murray, David. 1987. They love me and I learn: Frank Hamilton Cushing and ethnographic method. *European Review of Native American Studies* 1(2): 3–8.

Pandey, Triloki Nath. 1972. Anthropologists at Zuni. *Proceedings of the American Philosophical Society* 116(4): 321–37.

Parezo, Nancy J. 1985. Cushing as part of the team: the collecting activities of the Smithsonian Institution. *American Ethnologist* 12(4): 763–74.

Stevenson, Matilda Coxe. [1904] 1970. *The Zuni Indians: their Mythology, Esoteric Fraternities, and Ceremonies.* Reprint. Glorieta, New Mexico: Rio Grande Press.

Truettner, William H. 1985. Dressing the part: Thomas Eakin's portrait of Frank Hamilton Cushing. *American Art Journal* 17(2): 48–72.

# Photography Credits

| | |
|---|---|
| frontispiece | Batista Moon, ©'93. |
| page 106 | Edward S. Curtis, ca. 1903. |
| page 119 | John Hillers, ca. 1880. |
| back cover | Ben Wittick, ca. 1885. |

# Acknowledgments

The A:shiwi A:wan Museum and Hertiage Center is grateful to the Institute of the NorthAmerican West, Paper and Gold (Stateline, Nevada), and Dennis and Barbara Tedlock for contributing to the costs associated with this book.

Special thanks to Nigel Holman, Executive Director of the A:shiwi A:wan Museum and Heritage Center, for his behind-the-scenes work in collecting and organizing materials for this book.

# Publishers

The A:shiwi A:wan Museum and Heritage Center (AAMHC) was created in 1990 after almost thirty years of discussion and planning. Its museum and archives-based programs of research, exhibition and outreach operate using the so-called "eco-museum" approach in which the community controls the planning, implementation and dissemination of activities coordinated by a staff of professionals drawn primarily from the community itself. The operations of the AAMHC are overseen by a board of directors comprised exclusively of tribal members.

As part of our plans for long-term stability, we are applying for a National Endowment for the Humanities Challenge Grant which will provide a 1:3 match for an endowment of $1million established by the Zuni Tribal Council. As part of this grant, the AAMHC's share of net proceeds from the publication of this book will also be matched by the National Endowment for the Humanities.

A:shiwi A:wan Museum and Heritage Center
P. O. Box 1009
Zuni, New Mexico 87327
505-782-4403

For more than a hundred years Zuni craftsmen have been making jewelry and pottery for sale to traders. For at least fifty years the Zuni Tribe has wanted to start its own business to market Zuni arts and crafts. In March of 1984 Pueblo of Zuni Arts & Crafts was founded as a tribal enterprise charged with developing markets, new crafts, shows, and publications about Zuni arts. To that end, Pueblo of Zuni Arts & Crafts has created a wholesale network which stretches across the United States to Europe and Japan. It also has art galleries in San Francisco, Los Angeles, and Zuni.

Phil Hughte's book of Cushing cartoons is part of this effort to showcase Zuni Artists. A book on pottery and another on fetishes are currently in print. A Zuni jewelry book is also being written.

Pueblo of Zuni Arts & Crafts
P. O. Box 425
Zuni, New Mexico 87327
505-782-5531

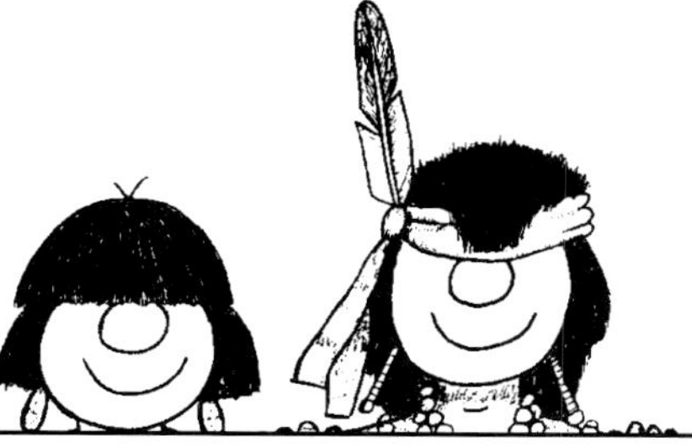